GIRL
LEAST LIKELY TO

GIRL
LEAST LIKELY TO

Thirty years of fashion, fasting and Fleet Street

Liz Jones

**SIMON &
SCHUSTER**

London · New York · Sydney · Toronto · New Delhi

A CBS COMPANY

First published in Great Britain by Simon & Schuster UK Ltd, 2013
This paperback edition published in 2014
A CBS COMPANY

Plate section
p.8: top left © Ken McKay / Rex Features;
bottom left © Fiona Hanson / Press Association;
bottom right © IPC Media.

1 3 5 7 9 10 8 6 4 2

Simon & Schuster UK Ltd
1st Floor
222 Gray's Inn Road
London WC1X 8HB

www.simonandschuster.co.uk

Simon & Schuster Australia, Sydney
Simon & Schuster India, New Delhi

A CIP catalogue record for this book
is available from the British Library

Paperback ISBN: 978-1-47110-196-0
eBook ISBN: 978-1-47110-197-7

The a ct

Pri

For my mum

CONTENTS

About the Author

Liz Jones is Fashion Editor of the Daily Mail, and a columnist for the Mail on Sunday. She is the former editor of Marie Claire, which sounds quite an achievement, but she was sacked three years in. A psychotherapist once told her, 'What you brood on will hatch', and she was right. Nothing she ever did in life ever worked out. Nothing. Not one single thing.

This memoir chronicles Liz's childhood in Essex, the youngest of seven children with a mum who was both a martyr and disabled, a dad so handsome and dashing no other man she ever met lived up to his impossible pressed and polished standards. Her older brothers were hippies or, as her dad called them, long-haired layabouts, bloody hooligans. Liz was not like her siblings. They terrified her, with their Afghan coats, cigarettes, parties, sex and drugs. They made her father shout, and her mother cry. She was, is, painfully shy, and became a borderline anorexic aged 11, having been force-fed brown bread toast and homemade marmalade by her mum since birth, which she learned was bad for her in the pages of her sisters' *Petticoat*, and *Cosmopolitan*, *19* and *Honey*. In 1975 Liz discovered *VOGUE*. From then on, it was always, always *VOGUE*.

Liz's start in journalism did not augur well: her first proper job was at *Lyons Mail*, staff of two, the newspaper for employees of Joe Lyons & Sons' tea shops and factories, during which she was forced to wear a hair net and blue plastic covers on her shoes. After a few halcyon years on *Company* magazine, during which she compiled a pop quiz and was sent to review a spa on the English Riviera, she then spent several dark years on the weekly magazine *Woman's Realm*, where she attempted to learn to knit her own Christmas pudding, and tied the entire population of post-menopausal British women in an impenetrable knot with her lack of attention to detail. At last, she made it to Fleet Street, where she put a curse on designer Ossie Clark for almost getting her sacked from *The Sunday Times Magazine*, and later upon the glossy, double-headed hydra of Demi Moore and Ashton Kutcher, who invoked a very Leveson assault on Liz's email box, the trauma of which she has yet to recover from.

She was named Columnist of the Year 2012 by the British Society of Magazine Editors (the BSME awards, known colloquially as the Mad Cow gongs), but spoiled the moment by tripping up the stairs to accept the award in her cream, spangled Louboutins and over-long, strapless, Bottega Veneta dress that refused to stay up, given Liz had her pendulous, NHS-propagated breasts cut off aged 30. She was heard to mutter, as she posed for photos accepting the award, arms clamped to her sides to prevent exposure of her transplanted nipples (the plastic surgeon had to relocate them, for all the world as if he were Phil Spencer), 'How does Sarah Jessica Parker do it? How?'

The not-so-private life is all here, too: she remained a virgin until her thirties, and even then found the wait wasn't really worth it, as the sex wasn't good; she found it tiring, just one more thing to add to her 'to do' list. Anyway, she is too repressed to ever really let go. She doesn't enjoy being seen naked from different angles. She is famously barren – her womb, despite the posters of Paul Newman and David Cassidy on her bedroom wall and the decades of longing, has never been used. Perhaps she could take it back? She lives alone with her four rescued collies (Michael, Jess, Grace Kelly and Mini Puppy), three horses and 17 cats, including Susie, Sweetie, Minstrel, Leo, Boy and Mummy Cat, in an undisclosed location. Despite three decades of Pilates and much plastic surgery, she still has a stress-fat tummy. She has been called 'the Queen of confessional journalism' by Radio 4, has three million dedicated readers of her column about her so-called life in the *Mail on Sunday*'s *YOU* magazine, but is still too frightened to answer the telephone, too filled with disgust at her own image to ever look at her byline photo, or listen to her voice, or glance in the mirror, or eat a whole avocado. This book is the opposite of Having It All, and makes a mockery of the shiny-haired L'Oreal mantra, 'Because I'm Worth It'. It is a life lesson in how NOT to be a woman.

'My girls are the vertical owners of mink coats'

Norman Parkinson

'Didn't you think it strange he was married, but still couldn't get a date on New Year's Eve?'

Diane Keaton, talking about Woody Allen's character in *Play It Again, Sam*

Introduction

'I'M GETTING BETTER. THANK YOU'

I went to visit my mum today. She is in her old bedroom, still in the semi-detached Sixties' house she shared with my dad in Saffron Walden in Essex, but the room could now be any-where. Or at least, anywhere inside an institution. Her bedroom furniture has been taken away – the double divan, the heavy, dark dressing table – as the carers found it to be in the way, too low, too high, too heavy. Basically, my mum's pride and joy, Pledged over many decades, contravened health and safety. She is, instead, in a narrow hospital cot, with metal bars on each side, a hoist above her hovering like an obscene child's mobile. It twinkles, I suppose, when some-one has bothered to open the curtains (a ritual that began and ended my mum's every day, while she could still wield a mop to shove the heavy, oak curtain pole back up into place, given it always drooped with the weight of the blue velvet). But rather than being a comfort, the mobile-hoist hybrid is a constant reminder of her infirmity.

Everything in the room is the colour of her dentures, which she no longer wears, given she no longer eats solids. There are pads and wipes and cotton wool and anti-bac gels everywhere, as though she were a giant baby. She is served tiny spoons of baby food by a Latvian carer who shouts, from time to time, 'How are you feeling today, Meesees Jones?' A lifelong tea addict, her only liquid is lukewarm water, syringed from a small pipette into her gaping maw; a mouth like that of a long-neglected baby bird. Occasionally, the water hits the back of her throat and she splutters. She can no longer watch TV, even if she could ever find her glasses (a lifelong quest), or listen to the radio, so these last ornaments of normality have been excised. She doesn't really know it is me, her youngest child, her baby, her Lizzie (her other children were summoned with a roll call – ClarePhilipNickLynTonySue – until she hit upon the right one, but she always knew it was me) sitting by her bed, my silver laptop a shield from her torment.

I sit watching her. She keeps rubbing her pin head (as a child, she always reminded me of Mrs Pepperpot, her neat, grey bun secured with brown grips) from side to side, so I set aside my laptop and bend over her, scratching the back of her head. It must be that feeling I get when I am prone on a mas-sage table, and my hair has sat in one place for too long on a folded, fluffy towel. Her left eye is closed, stuck fast with a sort of glue. Having finished the head scratch, my mum now turns her head to look at me with one eye open, still bright blue. She reminds me, a lifelong fashionista, of a cover of *i-D* magazine, in which every celebrity is shot with one eye artfully, inventively obscured. I bet they've never thought of nonagenarian eye glue.

As my mum peers at me, Kate Moss fashion, she doesn't say, 'Who the hell are you?', as she has politeness ingrained into her core, like words in a stick of rock, but she is thinking those words, I'm sure. There is no glimmer of recognition, no indication that she knows it is me, her 'darling'. When the live-in carer and her thrice-daily helper, a girl who looks barely 18, turned my mum on her side to wash her this morning, I saw her back and it appears to be rotting, or at least disintegrating, as though she had been drowned at sea some time ago and has only just been beached on the shore of the NHS. The pain must be considerable but all my mum will murmur to the carers when they place an ear to her mouth is, 'I'm getting better. Thank you.'

She is obviously made of a substance they stopped producing after 1921.

My mum spent all her life working hard: polishing, cooking, mangling, pegging, ironing, pressing, weeding, whisking, Vim-ing, kneading, mixing, mincing (not an affectation, but what you used to do, by hand, to yesterday's Sunday joint), rubbing fire tongs, pokers and door knockers with old Marks knickers soaked in Brasso, and cutlery with Silvo. And she never once lost her temper with anyone, despite the endless tasks and arthritis. She was patient and self-sacrificing. She never swore, raised her voice, or had a piercing. She never owned a pair of trainers or shaved her underarms or legs, or wore sunglasses, or any garment with an elasticated waist. She couldn't drive a car, didn't even write a cheque until after my dad died ('Cashback? What's that, Dear? Ooh, how marvellous!'). She never had an affair. She was never greedy. The tradition in our house, if we children were working our way through the Quality Street tin at Christmas, was that she wouldn't take her own sweet but would wait, like a well-trained Labrador, until one of us spat ours out with disgust (one with a coffee-flavoured middle, say, or a jelly centre). She would eat that one for us, to avoid waste. If, while she was still sentient, I took her flowers or a box of Bendicks chocolates (I was nothing if not upwardly mobile), at the end of the visit she would always press the gift in my hands, insisting I take it home with me. If I took her fresh peas, she would pop them straight in the freezer. My mum was never about 'now', she was always about tomorrow or, more accurately, the day after tomorrow.

And look where that attitude has got her now. I show her the tulips I have just brought her: 'I'm so lucky,' she whispers. 'Thank you.'

Look, I think, peering at her hollow eye sockets, her open mouth, her fingers with their overlong nails still bearing her mother's diamond engagement ring, where being good for 93 years has got her. A decade alone in a narrow single bed.

Before I leave her that day, I look around downstairs for a bit, mainly for something to do as I find it hard to sit next to her for long periods at a time, holding a hand that is now so soft when as a child it was always rough and scaly from washing up without Marigolds ('Oh, I don't need them'), a texture that meant our hand-knitted sweaters and tank tops were always prematurely pilled. I walk through the rooms, opening cabinets in 'the lounge' that had been her pride and joy, always buffed, looking at her lifetime collection of things that are now all worth so little, and probably always were. Her pale-blue-and-white Wedgwood plates and ornaments, crystal vases that rarely, if ever, held fresh flowers, my dad's silver cufflinks and broken Parker pen, the clock on the mantelpiece that was always slow, or fast, ancient cookery books in the kitchen with black-and-white photos that, as I flick through them, bring back memories of childhood: the Victoria sponge, the rock cakes. Those bloody rock cakes. All I wanted as a child were fairy cakes decorated with silver balls but Mum couldn't afford silver balls; maybe every now and then a Lyons Swiss roll but it was never adulterated with the frivolity of cream, not even buttercream.

I open a drawer in the kitchen and there are the implements my mum used all her life: a rolling pin with one handle missing, a blunt potato peeler. Still, now, and rusting. Around the room there are brown tiles depicting ears of corn that, after 25 years in this rented house, my parents never thought to remove and change for something better, something a bit more tasteful. The tiny, twisted, fake Christmas tree under the stairs is gone, though, along with the three-dimensional foil star edged with tinsel that I made, having carefully followed the instructions on *Blue Peter*. It was thrown away last summer when my mum was given weeks, if not days, to live. If my mum survives until next Christmas, she won't even have that gaudy monstrosity on the cabinet by her bed to remind her of the years she spent hot in the kitchen, roasting a capon. (I only found out recently that a capon is a big male chicken. We never once had turkey, as turkey was 'too expensive'.)

On the massive hulk of a sideboard with its stack of board games (the chess set had all the tops of the knights and monarchs chewed off by our dog Pompey in his early years) are photos not of us, her seven children, but of her many, many grandchildren and great-grandchildren: 19, approx., at the last reckoning; I've simply lost count. 'We didn't really have cameras in those days,' was my mum's answer when I had queried the lack of evidence of our childhoods. As a teenager, I had vaguely thought I must have been adopted. I open the tallboy and find an old Viyella shirt box. I open it to find it's full of my magazine and newspaper clippings, all in date order, every single one, or at least until 1999 when my mum's brain stopped even though my writing didn't. My mum never told me she had read or seen anything I had written: my parents didn't overly go in for praise. In the Eighties, when I told them I was going to Los Angeles to interview New Jack Swing star and future husband of Whitney Houston, Bobby Brown, my mum phoned me not to say, 'Well done, you are the first member of our family to go to the United States'; instead, I heard my dad's clipped, Art Deco tones by her side warning me the place was riven with gang crime. But she was proud, it turns out, that I had done slightly more than just avoid being run over by a green number 11 bus on the A130 from Chelmsford to Southend seafront. Maybe that makes the past 30-odd years of my career all worth it. But no. Not quite. As we shall see.

There was one moment of hilarity, though, during my visit. The carer told me Mum had been calling out in the night. 'Robert! Robert!' she had wailed. 'Where are you, Robert?' The carer said she had tried to calm her down, saying, 'There IS no Robert. You are dreaming! There IS no Robert!'

No one had thought to tell the carer the name of my poor mum's dead husband.

Walking back upstairs, turning sideways as I have had to do for more than 15 years due to the Stannah stairlift (my dad would trot up the stairs with his lead hand outstretched, grasping an imaginary partner in a faux tango), I realise that every single thing my mum told me growing up, what she taught me with her stoicism, her uncomplaining nature, her *nice*ness, was just not true. Things will not be okay. Things will not come right if I am patient. Life is not cosy as long as the fire is lit and the cheese and biscuits are on the tray and the salt cellar hasn't fallen over yet again. Because if my mum, after a lifetime of sacrifice, of gentleness, of hard work and selflessness, can be condemned to a decade and more spent prone in her size 18 floral M&S nightie (the other week, a temporary carer, drafted in because the full-time one was on holiday, put on a clean nightie that was slightly too small and it chafed around my mum's arms, giving her red weals: how odd, I thought, watching the Sudocrem be slathered on to the wound, that something so homely and full of mummyness as a Marks winceyette nightdress could be so easily turned into an instrument of torture) with not even any thoughts scudding past her closed eyes to keep her company, then what hope the rest of us? If there are any thoughts remaining in my mum's small head, such as whether she's remembered to get the washing in, or picked the mint for the mint sauce from the clump by the washing line, or aired the tea towels, or 'done the fire', or proved the dough, or made a list, or asked Daddy, she finds them so confusing as to be frightening, as she hasn't completed any of them at all.

Who would guess that behind that ordinary front door, in this ordinary house, is something so extreme in its awfulness – worse than Guantanamo Bay, worse than anything else I can think of. How strange that home, which was the only place I was told was safe for me to inhabit, should be a house of horrors. It was always the *outside* world my mum and dad wanted to protect me from. Even when I was grown up, if I told Dad I was planning to go somewhere, he would map the route, then telephone me, telling me the journey I was about to take was 'extremely dangerous'. If I cycled from the rectory in Rettendon along the A130 towards Wickford, a barren place but it had a Woolworths, Millets, library and tennis court, I would be warned 'The A130 is the most dangerous road in Essex.' Even now, jaded and having landed in a foreign clime, my first reflex is to reach for my phone and let my dad know I've arrived safely. Three rings (my parents had no truck with unnecessary expensive telephone calls) meant I'd arrived and not been murdered. I imagine any sort of pro-longed silence sent them into a spin.

Often, as I sit by Mum's bed in a dreadful chair that also doubles as the commode she can no longer even sit on, she turns her one eye to me and it is leaking tears. As a child my biggest fear was that my mum would die, but more than once over the last few years I have considered smothering her with her embroidered pillow. Anything to end her torment. I used to pray for my parents every night: 'Please help my mum, dad, Penny [the rabbit], Guinea [the guinea pig] and Pompey [the randy, flatulent Labrador-Retriever cross].' I would have to open and close my hands in prayer a certain number of even times, enacting a solitary game of paper, scissors, stone (an OCD tic that continued until I was married but stopped when my husband found my nightly prayers comical and then annoying). If I didn't pray and count, pray and count, someone close to me would die. I always assumed my mum would topple first, as she seemed the most vulnerable. She was always an invalid; I never knew her as anything else. When I was 11, she went 'into Broomfield', a ghastly hospital just outside Chelmsford, to have her neck stretched to help with the pain of arthritis. My dad had to cook while she was away: poached egg in mashed potato. I still can't eat either.

She had numerous operations: new knees, new hips. Often, she would develop a life-threatening blood clot, which meant she was prescribed 'anti-establishments' (coagulants) to thin her blood. She was always an old mummy, not the sort who would go shopping with you in Topshop, or buy you a bra. Now I wish my mum would die before the palliative care funding stops (you'd have thought, mistakenly, it ends with the grave, but no) and she is forced into a care home. She will be buried with my dad ('On top of him!' my oldest sister, Clare, said lewdly when we were discussing funeral logistics: how inappropriate, I thought. Mum simply doesn't do lewd) in the cemetery outside Saffron Walden, just before you get to the giant Tesco, and this ghastly prison sentence will be over. My mum doesn't want to go into a care home because she thinks Daddy will not be able to find her. After he died, in 1998, my mum says she saw him, downstairs in the hallway, young and handsome in his army uniform. She always wanted to see him again, so wouldn't dream of leaving the house, even though she is sentient in fleeting moments only.

No one has told Mum that her son, Nick, has died. We buried him in February 2011. The humanist service was held at a 'green' burial ground in Essex, just off the M25. Not the most romantic of locations, but everyone buried there gets a tree planted on top of them, along with wild flowers. Lyn's son, also called Nick, was by now too ill for her to travel home from Australia to be there, but Clare gave a eulogy. She called Pompey 'Popeye' and we all laughed at her mistake. Nick's body was in a cardboard, biodegradable coffin; it seemed tiny.

As he was wheeled outside into the biting wind, Monty Python's 'Always Look on the Bright Side of Life' crackled out of the speakers. It was a non-conformist funeral for a man who had never quite fitted the mould.

As well as Monty Python, Nick loved Bach and Bartók. After being sent down from university, he headed to London and, as well as playing with Cockney Rebel, Annie Lennox and Julie Felix, joined a couple of bands – Red Brass and Ascend. I remember seeing him on *The Old Grey Whistle Test*, head bent over his guitar, long, lank hair hiding his face. He didn't look up, once, so uninterested was he in fame, or so diffident, I'm unsure which. Some of his bandmates made it to the funeral. One had brought a review by Chris Welch of a gig Ascend had performed, which read: 'Equal in stature to some of the biggest names in American contemporary music ... slightly less eccentric than The Spoons.' All these names no one has ever heard of only serve to illustrate how elusive success is. Nick wasn't interested in money. He never owned a property or a credit card or held a driver's licence. At the funeral, a friend recounted how Nick had once gone into a branch of John Lewis, a tale as improbable as being told one of his singles had reached number one. I also found out that, when my brothers and sisters and I had chipped in to pay for our father's funeral, in 1998, Nick had sold his last guitar so that he could do his bit. Not selling out had its drawbacks.

Nick was admitted to hospital over Christmas and died shortly after New Year's Day. Having suffered from pneumonia, he seemed to be rallying, listening to England win the

Ashes, and reading the obituary of his contemporary, Gerry Rafferty. But then he came down with vomiting and diarrhoea, which made him the latest casualty of NHS spending cuts, meaning he'd been shunted from pillar to post until a bed in intensive care could be found. Because he'd been so cantankerous, no one had bothered to wheel him to the bathroom. What a small disease to fell such a big presence. He became a victim of the capitalist bastards after all.

Mum knows, though, about Nick, on some level. The other day, she told a new live-in nurse that she only has six children. She also said she saw my dad and her mum in her room, waiting for her. I hope that is true.

So, I sit with my mum, tapping away, writing this book. And, I suppose, when you are staring at someone with whom you used to watch *Ironside* (I had a thing for Ed, the tall, besuited sergeant who wore a narrow, black tie, given it was the Sixties), sharing a bar of Dairy Milk, and she is in such torment and you simply cannot help her, even though she has always helped you, then you inevitably take stock.

I wish I had been bad, just a little bit. Braver. Smoked a cigarette, say, or flirted with a man. Had a one night stand. Called in sick. Shown her I, too, could make a grandchild. Taken a year off, or perhaps just a week. Because good ends don't necessarily happen to nice people; it's the grabbing bitches who get the rewards, as I was to learn much later in life, too late. I was always cautious, probably because, having grown up in the Sixties and Seventies ('Forties, more like!' my

ex-husband used to say in one of his endless swipes at my
extreme antiquity), hearing about what my brothers and sisters got up to at the Isle of Wight festival, say (Tony set a
woman's afro alight when sparking up one of his endless rol-
lies), or in dreary bedsits in Tufnell Park with the curtains
permanently closed, terrified me. The danger! The conse-
quences! The heartbreak! My dad was always cross with them,
the long-haired layabouts. They made my mum cry.

I wish someone had told me, not that I was beautiful
because I know I'm not, but that I was normal and acceptable. Then, perhaps, I wouldn't have spent my life trying quite
so hard to be better than I am. Lying. Manipulating. Tanning.
Plucking. Jogging. Dieting. Staying late (in the office, not up –
I always knew I had to get my beauty sleep). I never once
disobeyed the glossy magazine mantra of 'Cleanse, tone and
moisturise!'

Maybe it was because my image in Mum's dressing table
mirror didn't measure up to the ones I saw in *Diana* and
Jackie and *Honey* and *19*. Aged ten I had made my own magazine, cutting photos out of Lyn's pile, and called it *Trendy*.
Twiggy was on the cover, in an unprepossessing striped tank
top, as I'd cut her out from the cover of *Vogue Knitting*. 'How
to get Twiggy's legs' was one feature: my answer had been 'to
wear fab white tights'. I wrote a list of banned foods. There
was a problem page, of course there was. I put the finished
magazine in the bottom of the wardrobe.

Maybe it was because all around me there was chaos: so
many other children and noise and untidiness, despite my

mum's best efforts to stem the tide. My mum loved me but was always too shy to say I looked lovely, Darling, or ever talk to me about things like periods or towels. Maybe this is why the anorexia started: I wouldn't have dreamt of telling my mum that I had started bleeding, not a mum with a darning box, a tape measure so worn you had to guess, and special built-up slippers (one leg was much shorter than the other).

But other people could have, should have, taken me as they found me – my husband, friends, boyfriends (that last word barely deserves a plural, as there were only three and one of those only lasted six months, so really it was two and a half men). But as I was always in doubt about my own right to be alive, how could they not be, too?

I wanted to be more exotic, like Marie Helvin or the woman with the buttock-length hair Marlon Brando fell in love with during *Mutiny on the Bounty*, not someone who had grown up thinking a box of Vesta Chow Mein (it was desiccated, so not even found in the cold aisle) was the height of sophistication. Someone who had nothing more to listen to in their small, grey, faux leather record case than 'The Holly and the Ivy' and Danny Kaye singing 'The Ugly Duckling'. My feathers were all stubby and brown.

But then, Essex was a bleak place to live, with only the local Wheatsheaf, slumped on the side of a dual carriageway, as a distraction. It's been boarded up now (I drove past the other day – even the dual carriageway has died! It has been grassed over, now the new bypass sears through fields that once held bright yellow gorse and chaffinches and yellowhammers). Essex is a different place these days, of course: women with skin the colour of The Three Degrees, the eyelashes of a drag queen, skirts up around their thongs, their haunches vajazzled. It wasn't like that in my day, I thought not long ago when I attended Essex Fashion Week in Rainham (oh, how my career has soared!) and watched the chattering queue outside the Tanfastic booth.

But at least these women are changing themselves because they think they deserve a bit of fun: men, kids, a gel manicure, white BMW 4x4. I wanted to change myself because I couldn't bear to be me any longer, someone who came from a kitchen with ears of corn embellished on the walls and a fake *Hay Wain* in the lounge. I didn't want to be like my mum, with a husband and seven children and not a moment to herself, who always fell asleep before the nine o'clock news, knitting on her knee. But then, perhaps, I did follow her example in one way. I took her determination to polish and just rubbed at things at work, at my own body, endlessly. (When I was first with my ex-husband, I wanted to be so much better for him, as a reward for him having married me. I left my house in Hackney one day and had my hair dyed, my eyelashes extended, an airbrush tan, teeth whitened, brows dyed so black I resembled Groucho Marx. When I got home he said, 'You look great. But I didn't expect you to return a member of a different ethnicity.')

I wish I could rub out my life, twiddling knobs as on an Etch A Sketch, and start again. I wish I had appreciated my mum while I still had her, not wailed about whether or not there was meat in the stew or lard in the dumplings, and why couldn't I have a fab chain belt from Bonds? How many years did I waste in a concrete bus shelter with its glass smashed, waiting for a number 11 bus, or Marlon Brando, to arrive, or for my life to start, whichever was sooner?

I think I would do every single thing completely differently.

Chapter one

I'M EITHER A PLATE OR A BOY

I remember the first time I knew I wasn't good enough. My mum had just Vosened my hair – a sort of Davy Jones bob, but nowhere near as shiny – in the kitchen sink. Our kitchen was a narrow cell, with a wall of heavy, scrubbed oak drawers and a teeny fridge in one corner: God only knows how it stored food for seven children and two adults. I suppose there were old Quality Street tins, too, that contained Rich Tea biscs. No dishwasher. No automatic washing machine. My mum did the laundry in a great big tub every Monday, surrounded by soft mountains of linen from eight beds, before squeezing it all through a hand-cranked mangle. There were bluebottles, circling, at all times of the year, due to the battery farm owned by the Littles family next door; we'd buy cracked eggs, as these were cheaper. Mum also bought the ones with thin skins that wobbled. Mrs Little assumed these defective eggs were for Pompey, but they were for us.

I always had my hair washed in this kitchen because there was a single bar electric wall heater, which my mum would put on when Dad wasn't looking. That day I was laughing, about what I can't imagine, but, as I did so, leaning over to stop water trickling down into my handmade scratchy plaid pinafore, always worn over a hand-knitted jumper made from wool unravelled from some other wretched garment (no one in my family took their clothes off, if at all possible, given the freezing temperatures, or bought a new, plump ball of wool with its label intact, like a non-festive paper chain), I chipped my two front teeth on the steel of the sink. 'Oh, Darling,' my mum said, not thinking to tell me off for mucking about, or to question why I was not being washed in a deep bubble bath full of plastic toys. 'Oh, dear.'

I ran upstairs: big, broad, dark oak stairs that curved upwards from the Antarctic hallway. There was an old leather sofa in the hall, but no one ever sat on it, which relieved Mum as it was one less thing to plump. The house, a gothic Victorian rectory, was far too cold to ever linger. Pompey always slept at the bottom of the stairs, so you had to step over his big, yellow form (he was a randy sod – his was the first and pretty-damn-near last willy I ever saw: pink, shaped like my mum's Yardley lipstick). Sometimes he would stagger to his paws just as you were performing this feat, which was awkward for my mum, by then almost crippled with arthritis, as she would momentarily mount him, incongruous, showing her thick darned tights and Marks & Spencer broderie anglaise knickers. Sometimes, Pompey would perform a violent shake head to tail, which my mum would say 'Almost knocked my teeth out!' The black Bakelite phone, our number, 3086, Biro'd on its chest, was on a console in the hall, but it never rang. We had a party line. I thought, aged five, that meant it might ring on people's birthdays. It didn't.

I went into my parents' bedroom. It had a little room off one corner, what would once have been the dressing room, which housed Tony, next child up after Sue: a ginger-headed, freckled, bandy-legged brother who decorated what was little more than a cupboard with Man United paraphernalia and blown wild birds' eggs (the sight of robin's egg blue still makes me mournful). I went to the bay window, overlooking the always half-mown lawn (my dad kept one half as 'rough'; I've no clue why) and the garden of the Littles (those richer, posher people who lived next door in our divided house – they got the big kitchen; ours was the old scullery – and who would sometimes throw rhubarb over the fence to us for pudding. It once struck me on the head). I sat on the red velvet stool in front of my mum's dressing table. There were her ivory-backed brushes and a pot that had once been full of face powder but was now empty bar cufflinks and paperclips, a blue china rose as its handle. My mum is the least vain person I have ever encountered. She would make her own dresses – usually floral tea frocks, with buttons down the front, called shirtwaisters. Mum was so self-sacrificing, she always refused anything new for herself and, as she never went anywhere and was so awkward with her hip, a hand-made wool skirt seemed adequate. Her only nod to frivolity on a hot Sunday when she'd sit on the wooden bench at the far side of the lawn, which she'd have staggered towards at an extreme angle with a wooden tray of tea, was to remove her stockings. She would never kick off her shoes, as her toenails were deformed by arthritis, like mini hooves. She only occasionally wore make-up – block mascara you had to spit on – but never had the unguents needed to remove it, let alone anything with which to moisturise. 'It wears off,' she would say to my dismay; and my dad would touch her cheek, 'As soft as the day I married her, aren't you, Mummy?' And she would giggle like a teen.

The day she returned home having had all her teeth out still looms large in my kaleidoscope of Mummy memories. She looked so different that Pompey failed to recognise her and barked like a maniac, hackles up beneath his silver choke chain. She was still only in her forties but already she was old, stooped, in constant pain. It didn't occur to me to ask why she had had this done. What about Dad fancying her? It was weeks before she could wear her dentures and, even then, she never bothered with the correct adhesive to keep them in place, or tablets of Steradent, so they soon became brown and ill-fitting, clicking as she talked. It was normal, apparently. Women having their teeth out. She had had so many children, perhaps that took its toll. There was never any discussion, no pleading by any of us, even by Dad, that she should not do it; no question of a cap or a crown, although

Dad had one. I'd see it, gold in his head, and wonder about it. He had a wardrobe of rather loud, silver-grey suits from Austin Reed – a bit 'spivvy', my maternal gran would say – polished brogues from Church's, and colourful silk ties from Jermyn Street. At weekends, he was never out of his pressed slacks, Viyella checked shirts and Austin Reed navy blazer, a polka dot cravat at his throat, exactly like the one worn by Cary Grant in *To Catch a Thief*. This sounds profligate but he wore that blazer for 40 years. The shirts had frayed cuffs. He'd complain about the coal bill but he'd go to the pub most nights. My mum never minded, though: she'd just wait for his return with a tray of cheese and water biscs (surely the ungodliest biscuit ever known to man), warming cocoa for herself. She never asked to go to the pub as well. She probably had too much to do.

I should have learned that love is not about beauty from the way my dad would bow to my mum and click his brogues together, when she spied him mowing the lawn as she shook a duster out the window. But I didn't. I looked in the mirror on that day with wet hair. Sunlight shone full on my face. I examined my now-broken front teeth. The dressing table had three mirrors: a big oval one in the middle and two narrow panels at each side. I angled the other two mirrors to get a better look at the damage. And I glimpsed my profile for the first time. How other people must see me when I am unawares. I was shocked. I looked again. My face was flat, not like other people's faces. Not like my big sister Lyn's, with her perfect upturned nose (a year older than Tony, she had the

21

almond face of Jenny Agutter; her only ambition when she grew up was to be a nurse, marry a doctor and be a mum). Not like Gillian's or Caroline's or Penny's, the girls who lived over the A130 in the council houses on Meadow Road. It was like a soup spoon, or a saucer. I had a pointy chin, ears like a toby jug and, from the side, I could see my face was like the new moon. The man in the moon. I'm either a plate or a boy.

I decided I would never look at my reflection again. And, on the whole, I haven't.

I was always ashamed to be one of so many children when I started school. Kids would titter and ask if my mum was a Catholic. It seemed dirty, to me, to have so many in a world where sex was never discussed. There were seven of us. Sue, Tony, Lyn and then Nick, a year older again, with Dad's Roman-nosed profile, big, round face and Jones ears that I have (they stick out and are huge, like France). Obsessed with music from an early age, he was a shy, cross boy with an allergy towards dairy and leading a normal life. A year and a half older is Philip: dark haired, angry. Growing up he was so much older than me, so terrifying in his moods, I rarely spoke to him, nor him me. And finally Clare, who never got over being the oldest and who had already left home and married by the time I was out of babyhood: a fantasist, but in a way that made her an optimist, too. 'I'm writing a novel,' she will say, now, when I call her, even though she and I both know she has neither a laptop nor the inclination. Sue was my only playmate, given she was just 18 months older than me. It might sound quite like the Mitford family setup, given the Labrador and the fact we lived in a freezing rectory, but it wasn't like that at all. The rectory was the only place we could all fit: a rented house with no central heating.

I was born on 5 September 1958 in St John's Hospital in Chelmsford, Essex. They should get a blue plaque. When I asked my mum some years ago for the exact time I was born, wanting to get an in-depth horoscope drawn up so that I could hopefully have something to look forward to, or place sandbags against, she said, 'I've no idea, Darling. We didn't really think about those things.' (My mother has also never owned a watch. When she needed to time something in the oven, she would use the big clock on the mantelpiece in the lounge.) There were no giant black-and-white billboards of my infant face on walls, or placed in silver frames on piano lids. No locks of hair in silver lockets, or tiny booties in aspic, or charts on walls showing growth spurts. I suppose by the time you have your seventh child it all becomes a bit been there, done that, boiled the terry nappy. I imagine I must have been a mistake, as my parents could not afford another child. I caused my mum more work. I don't remember my dad ever holding me, or hoisting me on his shoulders. I was placed in a corner and it was simply hoped I'd take.

I remember a very early birthday. I'm in bed, in the single divan, lights off, and Sue and Lyn have yet to come to bed. Dad comes in and he says, 'Happy Birthday, Darling.' He doesn't kiss me or hug me, we are not tactile like that. I always turned away from my mum's goodnight kiss, given the dentures. And, even though I had not been given a present all day, I said, 'Thanks for my presents.' 'Oh, good,' he'd said, standing in the light from the hall. Embarrassed, maybe. But he loved my mum, and I'm sure he loved me, even though a weekend outing usually meant being left in the car with a coke and a bag of crisps with its small blue parcel of salt while he was inside the pub.

Chelmsford is probably the least noteworthy place on earth: apart from St John's Hospital, it had the Chancellor Hall (site of concerts by notable Seventies gods including Kevin Ayers), a Bonds department store (now Debenhams), and a swimming baths (I would catch many a persistent verruca there in my formative years). Marriage's flour mill was under the flyover (my mum, despite the arthritis in her spine, shoulders and hands, baked all our own bread) and there was a cricket pitch. Perhaps that was why I was born there, given my family lived all the way over in Shenfield, near Brentwood, at the time. My dad loved cricket. I was probably born in Chelmsford just so he could catch a match.

My maternal grandmother, who I always suspected was Jewish, hailed from Brixton, loved watching the wrestling on TV, had a habit of saying, 'Ay? That's what 'orses eat', referred to my dad, who was christened Bertie but renamed himself Robert, as 'the toff'. He wasn't really a toff, but he was so good-looking, with a David Niven tache and a Cary Grant tan, that he probably believed he was destined for better things than living in a tiny semi-detached house in Shenfield with three boys and an ironing board squeezed into the box room. His mother, Granny Jones (I never found out her first name; it just didn't occur to me to ask), was from Terling in Essex, a still picturesque village just outside Chelmsford, and was one of 13 children. Most of them seemed to perish before adulthood: Little Willy (!) drowned in a pond; another was killed in the trenches. Great Aunt Nel never married, which should have acted as an early warning for me, given all she ever did with her life was embroider tablecloths. Aunt Nel lost her beau in the Great War and her once-curly hair went dead straight overnight with the shock.

Granny Jones, born in 1884, went into domestic service aged 14 and would regale me as a child with tales about her time cleaning the grates and polishing the brass of the local big houses. She would tell me about growing up in Essex, where the family kept their own pig and bees. Her account of the life cycle of the pig and the bees (what on earth did they eat? Honeyed ham?) traumatised me, given it was so brutal. Who knew they did that to bees: made them smoke and then killed them? And they would kill the pig in the garden, a long and Hardyesque exercise only for the stoic of stomach. No wonder Granny seemed so hard. It is strange my mum never told Granny to stop frightening me, given she was always in the kitchen kneading bread or boiling suet puddings in their tea-towel bonnets. I never loved Granny Jones, after that, with her permed silver hair and blackened teeth. We were never allowed to mention the *Titanic* to her, either, as she would immediately start crying. She never got over it. She didn't know anyone on board, but it loomed large in her memory, like a nautical 9/11.

I still have one of her cotton undergarments: she had an 18-inch waist. Not in later granny life, but as a teenage girl. As a child I put the camisole on, unable to do up the teeny, cloth-covered buttons with my giant hands across my tummy, swollen with stews and Topics and Bar Sixes and Walnut Whips and rock cakes. I tried to do it up at the waist, tie those cream ribbons, and thought how big I must be not to be able to fasten it. I hated myself: already slightly hard of hearing, with brown eyes too close together, those Gallic ears, that flat face. I hadn't yet heard of plastic surgery but I could try to change my flesh, surely? Make it melt away. Get thinner. That was something I could do, if I set my mind to it. The granny cami was an early gauntlet. I sincerely wanted to *fit*.

Granny married a Welsh coalminer who had come to London to improve himself by enrolling as a fireman. They lived for a while above Shoreditch fire station, before he got a job putting out blazes at the Gainsborough film studios (now 'executive apartments') betwixt Hackney and Islington, where the Will Hay comedies were made (the film *Where's That Fire?* presumably made Granddad rather nervous). They had three children – Les, Olive and my dad, born at home at the cottage in Terling – and were soon installed in a terraced house in Mill Hill, north London. Quite a leap, in one generation, from scullery maid to comfortable, home-owning suburbia. From 13 children to just three.

Granny Jones had the foresight to send my dad to

Hampstead School for boys, a public school, which is where he caught the posh accent and the cream cable-knit sweaters worn slung over his shoulders, though I doubt they paid the fees: he probably had some sort of fireman's son dispensation. Hence my dad, when he started courting my mum (she was christened Edna; I knew her as Mummy and my dad always called her darling, unless in company, when he became slightly more posh, and called her Nan, lips pursed beneath his tache in a sort of shy mew) during the first year of the war, in uniform, was always 'the toff'. My mum was his bit of rough, his Ginger Rogers, with a similar chignon. Her dad was the doorman of the Saunton Sands Hotel in Devon, an Art Deco masterpiece still standing to this day.

Mum left school at 14: the norm for a working-class girl in the Thirties. What was a bit more unusual was that she took ballet for a while, a contemporary of Margot Fonteyn. I have a photo of her on my desk, performing an arabesque. Mum never flew as high as the future dame: she was always only able to perform the splits with one leg forward, but not the other. The ballet teachers used to push her legs to the ground, causing a great deal of pain. It was the first sign of the invalid she would become. 'Nobody thought about it in those days,' my mum would say in answer to my outrage at her treatment by her teachers. She had an older brother and sister, Ted and Ginger, and a younger brother, Tony. Their lives were nomadic, given my granddad worked in the hotel business and never owned his own home. My maternal gran was tough: thin and wiry, like Desperate Dan's mummy, with dangling pearl earrings. Mum never spoke much about them and fell out with her sister over something. Even though my mum was so soft, so loving, so self-sacrificing, she had an inner core of steel that was capable of surviving anything: bringing up seven children with no help, no appliances. Living with a handsome husband whom all other women swooned over, and awful, swearing children who never helped, never fully flew the nest (even as an adult, when Tony went to visit Lyn in Australia, my bedridden mum paid the bill).

My parents met on a bus in 1939. Their first and probably only date less than a week later (everything was speeded up in the war years, like Sky+ x30) was to see *The Wizard of Oz* at the cinema. Then they got married, after just six months: he in his uniform, her in a patterned frock from Horrocks, a hat and stout shoes. There is just one photo of their wedding day, her arm through his. They didn't go on honeymoon because 'there was a war on'. If all romances happened this way, there would be no women's literature, no romcoms, no news-paper columns, no agony aunts. But then, it was 1940, Dad was stationed abroad and she didn't see him for the next three years. He was in the tank regiment and his main claim to fame was that he served with Terry-Thomas and the oiled and shirt-less man who banged the bronze gong at the beginning of every Rank film. Whenever a film from this studio came on the telly, he would tell us again. He was based mainly in Italy. My mum would get postcards from Rome with him sitting on the rim of a fountain in a jaunty beret and the message, 'Am very fit.' Yes, he most certainly was.

While he was serving in Italy with his chums from Hampstead School, his tank took a direct hit and only he survived. When, as a child, I tugged at his cardigan with its leather arms and buttons (he refused to call it a Beatles cardigan) and asked whether he had killed anyone, he would never tell me, but he would have tears in his eyes as he remembered his dead friends around him. (The only other time I saw him cry was on his 50th wedding anniversary, and we'd all clubbed together to buy our parents a holiday in Jersey. The last they'd ever take together. There is a photo of Mum on that vacation, standing straight, in a dress she had made herself, smiling.)

While he was away fighting the Germans (which, in practice, meant racing other officers – he was soon made captain – by open-topped Jeep from one end of Italy to the other and going to see the opera at La Scala), my poor old inflexible mum was trying not to live with Granny Jones in Mill Hill: my mum always felt Granny Jones was posh and disapproving. Her daughter, Olive, became a prototype for Hyacinth Bucket in her Mill Hill house with leaded windows and 'music room', her husband, Uncle Nobby (!) with a respectable job at the Bank of England, her children, Pam (my godmother, who bought me a copy of the Bible and a painting of a mare and foal) and John, were always dressed like something out of a Fifties children's annual. Mum preferred to stay with her own mother in Portsmouth, a prime target for the Nazi bombers, which is where she gave birth to Clare: at home, without any pain relief, without any bother. She made all her own baby clothes, knitting tiny outfits. She would write to my dad, but not that often and none of her letters survive. Perhaps he didn't keep them or, more likely, years later she used them to light the fire. There was no pining, just practicality. And postcards. Three-year-old Clare had no idea who he was when he got back, and bit him. Was my mum worried that Dad might have had an affair, I remember asking her not long after I learned my own husband had been seeing other women. 'No, not Daddy,' she said. 'Not in those days.' It never crossed my mum's mind she needed to put make-up on for my dad, or exercise, or dye her hair. She never went to a hairdresser, not once, not until after he'd died and a woman would come to the house to cut her hair and rasp her feet. It wasn't confidence. It wasn't not caring. Was it subservience, self-sacrifice? She never put her children before her husband, so why not put herself before us? She never once said, 'I'm having a bath.' Not once. I don't know when she bathed; I expect she used our water, edged with scum. There was never a time when she wasn't on call for a game of cribbage, or a sandwich, or to let Pompey out, or in. I always knew I didn't want to be like that. It all looked too tiring, having a husband and children. Just like Granny Jones had been, Mum was a domestic servant. I still can't fathom her: no one is that self-sacrificing, surely?

But she was right, in the end, about my dad. He never even looked at anyone else. Okay, maybe Sue Barker, who he persuaded, when he was working for the Blood Transfusion Service, to turn up and give blood.

*

Philip, Nick, Lyn and Tony followed Clare, in pretty quick succession. My dad had been demobbed after the war and was offered a chance to go to university, an opportunity afforded to all officers whose education had been so rudely interrupted. But with an expanding family to support, he accepted a job working for the Gas Board. The Jones family moved to the Potteries. It all looked pretty ghastly from the few tiny, creased, black-and-white photos kept in my mum's wardrobe. My parents got a bulldog, but it went into a mad frenzy in the garden and attacked Nick. He was put down (the bulldog, not Nick) but it is likely the brothers were over-exciting the poor thing. Philip and Nick were always at loggerheads: Philip would roll Nick up in a carpet, then beat it with a stick, and sit on him. I don't think Dad knew how to deal with the boys: used to army discipline, he found them unruly and lazy.

My mum went swiftly from lipsticked, balloon-sleeved Ginger Rogers lookalike, to having to look after five children on very little money. After the excitement and glamour of the war, my dad found England, with its rationing, impossibly grey and boring. Although my parents still did crazy things together, such as driving to an army buddy's wedding in a blizzard (something my dad would never have allowed me to do as an adult). But in the early Fifties, still young and sad-dled with children, my dad decided to re-enlist. He was offered various postings, but only one allowed him to take his wife and family. My mum said there was no question that that was the one he should take. My mum had no friends, had never had a job – her family was her world. And so, the posting my dad chose was East Africa. It was 1952 and the beginning of the British colonialist fight with the Mau Mau, led by Dedan Kimathi.

They flew in an army plane with hard seats along each side. It had to stop off in Malta to refuel. Finally, after 24 hours, they arrived in Nairobi. They were given a house with a tin roof and a veranda: the children would lie in their beds at night, listening to the sound of a leopard, clickety clacketing above their heads. My dad, now permanently and happily clad in pressed khaki shorts and matching stetson, would sit on the veranda, hitting poor unsuspecting tarantulas and scorpions into oblivion with a golf club. To this day, as some sort of Jones throwback, having seen my mum and dad and siblings do it even in decidedly non-exotic Essex, I upend and shake every shoe or wellie before I put it on, just as every opened food packet is secured with a wooden peg. The morality of the East African campaign was never discussed when the photo album came out and Mum would point to photos of the children's parties at Christmas, no mention of detention camps or forced labour. My dad did what his superior officers told him. My mum simply didn't do introspection. Just laundry.

But Mum was in heaven, having escaped wartime Britain, not long out of rationing, and arrived in a warm, colourful world. I think she knew getting married would give her a touch of exotica. She'd wanted to do ballet, not be a shop girl. She wanted a better life than a small terrace in Portsmouth or the Potteries. But the only access she had, without much of an education, or money, was to marry up. I still wonder what my dad saw in her, and I don't mean that in an unkind way. My mum was certainly good-looking, but I imagine Granny Jones, with her house in a posh part of London, would have wanted someone a bit racier for my dad, which he could have had, given his good looks. So my mum was always striving – to have the perfect home, give him an uncreased shirt – as she didn't quite have the wherewithal to give him glamour. (That part was me in my marriage: never good enough for my much younger husband, always trying to make life perfect for him, smooth the way, like a white-coated attendant, frantically smoothing the ice in a game of curling.)

But their marriage worked: she adored him, and there were no arguments, remarkable given his Welsh temper. My dad always drove, while she would sit, hands in her floral-sprigged lap, not even required to read a map. They always held hands. And the marriage worked best in the hot, high altitude of East Africa, and the humid coastal beaches of Mombasa. There was not a day when she would say she was cross with Daddy, when they wouldn't speak. She loved him till the day he died and refused to leave his side in bed, even though he kept her awake when he cried out in pain or confusion. She wanted for her four daughters what she had, but not one of us got it. Clare, divorced. Lyn divorced, too, having married a much younger man, an Australian she met while he backpacked round Europe. Sue never married. I married someone I thought I could control because I never wanted to be like my mum, so tired, so unable even to make a decision on her own, nothing in her big, brown purse bar a button.

Mum had an ayah called Josephine, who wore wonderful, colourful head wraps, and who cooked and cleaned and helped look after the children. It was the first time Mum had ever had respite, and she was able to go out with Dad in the evening, most often to the Officers' Mess. Dad wrote a postcard home to Granny Jones, via Forces Mail: 'Mum, One of the reasons Nan doesn't wish to leave Mombasa.' The picture on the front is of the Nyali Beach Hotel, Mombasa, East Africa. The imposing white building is surrounded by palm trees and sandy beaches. 'We walk along the beach to this hotel where there is an open-air dance floor. Love to all, Bert.'

Clare was, by this time, aged twelve, Philip was nine, Nick three and Lyn two. Clare was a blonde, curvaceous Lolita in cotton frocks with Fifties prom skirts. It was all pretty idyllic. G and Ts in the Officers' Mess. Tea dances. Long days on the perfect sandy beach. The children learned Swahili; my mum would still say, until dementia set in, '*Kudja hupay*', meaning 'Hurry up'. Lyn, a tearful child, prophetically dressed up in a nurse's uniform and would only eat *mayai* (boiled egg). The older ones went to high school in the back of a pick-up truck. As my dad went off on duty every day, he made a great show of taking his rifle with him: he figured his family were only in danger if there was a gun in the house. Another English family, neighbours, were massacred. At this news, my mum probably just put the kettle on. Clare, pushing a sibling in a pram, was mugged, jewellery ripped from her fingers; Bruce, our Dalmatian, must have been temporarily AWOL. One morning, Mum got a telegram, telling her that her younger brother, Tony, just 21 years old, had died in a motorcycle accident. But there was no self-pity, no wallowing. She certainly didn't fly home for the funeral. 'We just got on with things,' she'd say. And then Mum nearly died.

She developed a fever and, being who she is, dismissed it as nothing. She got worse and was admitted to the hospital, which was only a taupe tent. It turned out that she had somehow caught typhoid, most probably from drinking warm milk while worrying about everyone else. She never bothered to have her 'injections'. She got worse and worse, developing rigors: feverish periods of delirium. My dad would stand outside her window, a mere gap in the canvas, with all five children: Lyn would hold his hand, eyes puffy; Tony, aged two and extremely red (the colour sort of diluted as he got bigger), on one hip; Philip and Nick leaning on cricket bats; and Clare, one hand to her mouth. The nurses looking after my mum all fancied my dad, tragic outside in the red dust in his uniform with his enormous, ill-tempered brood. But, of course, he coped marvellously with Josephine doing all the hard work – the cooking and the cleaning and the endless laundry. He thought he would lose my mum, but then, he had lost so many people in the last few years.

The nurses were desperate for my mum not to make it so they could make a play for my dad. They would pinch her and refuse to change her sopping sheets, which became freezing late at night. Mum would boil like one of her suet puddings and then shiver, by turns. She didn't complain, or even tell my dad of her treatment: always the martyr. She was given the last rites. But, after six months, she rather miraculously survived.

The family were told to take a holiday in order for her to convalesce, so my dad got leave and they all spent time on the beach at Mombasa. My mum started the habit of a lifetime: a dress, stockings, shoes and a cardi worn on the beach at all times, plus an unswayable commitment to buttering rolls. One afternoon, the family left my dad, who had fallen asleep, sunbathing. His legs burnt so badly, they never grew hair again. Even aged 80, being bathed by an uncomprehending Filipino nurse on the cancer ward, he would tell her why his shins were as sheeny as an Essex girl's nether regions after a Brazilian.

There was danger all around and, probably because of this, everyone remained gin soaked. One afternoon, Josephine was suddenly arrested and taken away in an open truck: she was revealed to be a member of the Mau Mau. She was never seen or heard of again. I wonder Mum didn't try to find her, but she had that inner core of steel that made her only concerned for her family. Lyn cried for her nurse, though; her big, warm, multicoloured lap. The boys just turned to my mum and made her their servant again.

My parents were apparently still having sex, pretty remarkable given the rigors, the burns, the grief, the hangovers and the proximity to danger. My mum was taken into the army hospital, yet again, with terrible gynaecological problems. The army surgeon was about to perform a hysterectomy, given she already had five children. They opened her up and discovered she was pregnant with . . . twins. One had died, but one survived: Susan Honor was born a few months later in February 1956. My mum was closed up, and left with only one viable ovary. They told her she would never be able to get pregnant again. How close we came to not having me.

In 1957, the conflict ended and the family came home, by boat this time, a long, tortuous voyage during which my mum and Lyn were seasick but Clare, now a teenager, prowled the decks, flirting with the sailors. They bought a tiny house in Shenfield: 57 Oliver Road, which is where my mum brought me home to after I was born in Chelmsford. All I remember of this house is that the back lawn was a patch of bald, dry earth, given all the boys played cricket. When Sue started primary school, my mum would wheel me up Brentwood High Street to collect her. Sue, round, fair and bubbly, would promptly turf me out of the pram, so I had to walk. Despite popular belief, there are hills in Essex. I remember, too, we had a grey cat called Smokey who gave birth to kittens under the garage. That's it. That is all I remember about my time in Oliver Road.

Clare was, by this time, a shop girl in Selfridges, dating a man who drove a sports car and was tall and darkly handsome. None of us went to the wedding, but I've seen a sepia photo: she has a tweed suit on, with a fur collar, kitten heels and a blonde helmet of hair, like Dusty Springfield or Kathy Kirby. Everything is brown, even the cake. She would soon return to visit, small child in tow, thick legs, a pencil skirt, a resentful husband, but my dad was always a bit cold, disapproving.

We owned the house in Shenfield but, after I came along, it became far too small. My mum was exhausted. She would cook by day and after she got us all to bed she would then start on the pile of ironing. But Mum would have been content anywhere. Dad, with his trademark army march, and steel-capped brogues, needed room to fluff out his *Times* newspaper, behind which he would sit crossly, occasionally giving it a shake.

And so my dad, demobbed, was by now working for the Blood Transfusion Service as a regional organiser, which meant not much money but that he was in charge of blood drives, visiting factories to persuade local workers to sign up. He sold the house in Shenfield and rented Rettendon Place, just seven miles south of Chelmsford. It had an enormous sitting room with brown marble fireplace, dining room with white marble fireplace, playroom and seven chilly bedrooms. It had one bathroom on the first floor, another on the top floor. The top floor was pretty much never used, apart from housing the bedrooms of Nick and Philip. The spiders on the top floor frightened me: giant bastards who never seemed to want to catch any flies. And Nick frightened me. He was into 'his music' and owned a cassette machine. Two big brown spools would rotate on this machine, and he guarded it with his life. He also had a harmonica, wet with spittle, and a brown guitar with a golden rump like Guinea's. He could mend anything, so my mum was always calling on him to change a plug or fiddle with the brown-cloth-bagged Hoover. He became very cross when I could not tell the difference between Donovan and Bob Dylan. But he had a kind heart. He bought me my first ever LP: the Monkees' first album, which had a glossy white cover, the name spelt out in the shape of a guitar. When it developed a scratch, I felt my life was over. It was the one, nice, new thing I had.

Dad had ideas above his station, given those halcyon years of military conflict. He wanted the big lawn to mow, the walled garden, the drive, but he didn't realise or think about what it would all cost to run. Our inaugural Christmas at Rettendon Place was the first, and last, when Dad splashed out: the small profit from Shenfield was swiftly spent. We went to see the Christmas grotto at Gamages in London. My dad bought an enormous tree and we all had presents. Christmas Day was the one day a year we used 'the lounge' in winter. It was simply too big to heat the rest of the time, which meant, come autumn, we decamped to 'the dining room' next door, which had a great big mahogany table my dad had bought at auction, so the sofa and chairs had to be squeezed round the sides. The boys were given building bricks with tiny trowels, Lego and Meccano, a chemistry set with iron filings, litmus paper and tiny test tubes. A table tennis table (although the white ping pong balls were soon deflated by Pompey) and Scalextric. Sue had a doll, Simon, a wretched, plump, blond thing with gingham drawers. I hated Simon. I got a rocking horse, a dapple grey with a red velvet saddle I named Silver. I was also given a book with drawings about a girl with long hair who rescues a Shetland pony and puts him in her car. I told Tony, who always wore grey school uniform shorts, that I could tell him the story, if he liked. 'You know it off by heart,' he said. I do! I thought. I love Shetland ponies. 'No, "off by heart" just means you have learned it by reading it over and over again.'

Because there were so many of us, and I was the youngest, I started to develop ways to cope with the noise, and the queues for the bathroom. At that first Christmas in the big house, I began to be extra careful about things, since they could so easily have been lost in the great big scrum. I was given so few things that each individual object became ultra special. I unwrapped my gifts and made a very careful pile on a chair, which I then guarded. I was never a careless child, leaving things lying around, in case someone else felt they were theirs, or broke them. Whenever I let my rabbit Penny out of her cage in the garage, I pasted notes on all the doors, telling people not to let the dog out.

But I saw, from beneath my fringe, my older brothers and sisters swearing, listening to loud music, growing their hair, making my dad watch *The Old Grey Whistle Test* when he wanted to watch the news, and I knew that I had to be good, that I must never upset Daddy. Every Friday, we would run out of food, and my mum would make Russian salad: white rice with frozen peas. All my brothers and sisters would moan and ask for more, and raid the biscuit tin, and say, 'What about pudding? Why didn't you buy Arctic Roll?' But I never did. My mum had a trick called 'half and half', which meant she would water down the milk. We often had folded pieces of newspaper instead of Izal toilet paper. She scrimped so my dad could still play the ex-pat. We had a crystal decanter, but it was always empty.

My mum had no control over my brothers or my sisters, but she never really tried. She never once raised her voice, or insisted one of us do something. Clare says she was smacked, but I don't believe her. Mum to me was a lap, endlessly safe and soft. I was scared of my dad, mainly because of the shouting matches he had with my brothers: he and Philip once had a fistfight, right before Sunday lunch. When the boys were teenagers, Mum woke early once, convinced they were hurt (my mum was always quietly convinced she had a sixth sense). She ran into the boys' room to see Philip asleep, blood on his pillow. He'd been involved in some fight and returned home late. She cleaned him up and boil-washed the pillowcase before my dad could find out.

Clare said Dad had mellowed by the time he got to me and Sue. He was so much older. Maybe the fight had left him. I once broke the dining room window by throwing a stone. We sat at the dining table and my dad noticed the crack. 'Who has been playing cricket? Oh, my godfathers!' My mum told him a large bird had flown into it. She would always protect me. But when someone is soft, others use that softness. Sue was a force to be reckoned with, she often

41

seemed hysterical, screaming, crying and, as far as I could make out, she seemed to play my parents off against each other. She would be difficult with my mum, then make sure she had stopped before my dad returned. She would be coy with Dad, but would tell my mum she needed to clean her dentures with Steradent. Once, Sue really wanted the Wings album and asked Dad to get it for her. It was warped and so she asked him to return it, which he did. But when he got there they had run out of Wings and so he came home with a copy of the soundtrack to *The Boy Friend*, which was mostly sung by Twiggy. Sue wasn't sure how to react: if she lost her temper, then Dad would realise Mummy was right about Sue's rages. If she just said thank you, she would have to listen to Twiggy. She said thank you. We all walked on eggshells around Sue, upon the hot coals of her temper. My mum wouldn't deny her anything; it wouldn't occur to Mum to say no to any of us. Sue's passage through puberty was like a ship rounding Cape Horn in winter. It was like having a poltergeist in the house but, instead of a ghost, I found her a dark, volatile presence. I often think Sue was jealous of my mum, having my handsome dad.

Nick, born in 1949, was by now in a lot of trouble. He had been expelled from Brentwood School for refusing to take part in the Saturday morning military exercises, when all the boys would dress up in uniform. He clashed wildly with my dad, who was aghast at a son who grew his hair long, wore a grubby white Afghan coat, even in bed, and smoked pot. In 1968, he got into Essex University, its rancid students at the vanguard of anti-Vietnam war protests. His non-conformist attitude, drug taking and propensity to liberate the student bar of its liquor precipitated a police raid of the student dorm tower block. Nick made the *Daily Telegraph*, and the university chancellor, Albert Sloman, succeeded in expelling him. I'd been so pleased when he'd left home. He was inscrutable. He was cool. He made me feel what I was, which was provincial and stupid. Whenever one of us younger ones had chickenpox or measles or a bad earache, he would walk around in a surgical mask, using only his elbows to open doors. He was even against me watching telly. 'But you listen to the record player,' I told him. 'But not to the same record, at the same time, as everyone else in the country.'

My dad was apoplectic that Nick had been sent down. No one told me what was going on, of course. I was barely ten years old, so no one thought I would understand. There would just be arguments every Sunday, right before the roast, about greasy hair, or loud music, or the fact Tony had had a party while they were out, or that Philip was spending so long in the bathroom. My mum, face red and hot from the oven, spatters of Yorkshire pudding batter in her bun, would try to placate everyone, to no avail. I still get nervous at the smell of spitting fat and simmering peas. I cannot stand conflict; I will avoid it at all costs. Like my mum, I do anything to smooth the ice.

Lyn, lovely Lynnie, only two years younger than Nick, was into the Beach Boys and the Beatles. She moved out of our shared room and into the room next to Nick, in the attic. She had tiny glass giraffes on her mantelpiece and an apricot beauty product, with a furry apricot as a handle, like a tiny pair of buttocks. She had long legs and muscular thighs. She had started reading *Cosmo* and *Honey* magazine (strapline: 'Young, gay and get ahead') and she'd lie on the brown sofa in the hall while Sue and I grabbed the ping pong bats from the playroom and battered her thighs and bottom, because one of the articles had said that it would disperse the fat. I don't know whether it worked but it was an early lesson: you have to suffer to be beautiful.

By the end of the Sixties, Clare had two children: Matthew and David, or 'Did', who was a plump, round-faced child. Lyn would go to stay with Clare, to babysit, so that she, her husband and their friends could go out to the pub. I don't know what might have happened between Clare's husband and Lynnie – again, I was too young at the time to understand the family politics – but I think perhaps there was a flirtation. I do know that Lynnie came home upset but was told by our mum to keep quiet about it. If Daddy had found out he would probably have gone mad at everyone involved, and my mum was all about protecting Daddy. Always the peacekeeper. Always the one with the worries. But, of course, Clare found out, because Lyn, tearful, told her. I never really knew if Lyn wanted what Clare had, or if she just got swept away. I doubt Clare's husband was solely to blame, and Lyn's beauty was obvious to anyone who looked at her.

No wonder I never flirted, or risked being drunk, given the havoc attraction caused in the lives of the women around me.

Both Clare and Lyn always seemed interested in men. They flirted. They giggled. They both had breasts. They were competitive. Sue was briefly into boys, but never had posters on her wall, or crushes. But me, with my flat face and white pop socks? I was never jealous of them. I never aspired to be like them, or wanted to be pretty and chased by boys. I never wanted a doll like Simon. I just wanted to be invisible. I equated having breasts with upsetting my mum by getting pregnant. I saw what the presence of men did to Lyn and Clare: turned them into people who simpered, coquettish, competitive. Why would you want male attention, what good did it do? I knew that I wasn't like my sisters, but neither did I want to be like my mum, a doormat, a tea towel. Mum would be in the kitchen, writing her shopping lists – half a Q, toms, biscs, pots (she abbreviated everything and never know-ingly bought anything that was 'whole') – for Mrs Manders', the grocers. She would limp there each day, wincing with every step. I never thought to carry her shopping for her, as I skipped along in the brown velvet hot pants with braces she had made for me aged six or seven (even then, I'd pull them down to cover my thighs). I never thought to help my mum because she was just *there*.

From a very young age, I knew I did not want the life my mum had. She was our servant: she lived only for us. She had no time to herself. And what did she get in return? Rudeness and worry. I didn't want what Clare had, either: a modern semi with carpet tiles and endless strawberries she froze and turned into purée.

And Lyn, once she had left secondary school, got a job in the wool department of Dickins & Jones – not something I aspired to, either. Our Auntie Olive, a hairdresser on Oxford Street and therefore with 'connections', secured her the job, which meant she had to catch a train from Wickford to Liverpool Street every morning. She eventually became bored with knitting patterns and ply, so she decided to become a nurse, training at Billericay Hospital, about 12 miles from home. With few or no qualifications, it was her only means of leaving home. Her main ambition was to marry a surgeon, or at least an anaesthetist. She left Rettendon Place to live in the nurses' home ('nursing home', she'd call it), to return on her days off with a guitar, her upturned nose covered in freckles, and a mysterious, long-haired boyfriend in tow. Lyn had a number of boyfriends; some of them were indeed doctors. She was so pretty and attracted so much attention, but her looks only seemed to bring her grief. A decade or so earlier, she would have had propriety to protect her. Now, she only had *Cosmo*. My dad just couldn't understand where he had gone wrong.

Philip, who had resented being plucked from his ex-pat high school in Africa and deposited in a dreary secondary modern, became, as he progressed through his teens, hot tempered, distant. I don't remember him saying one civil word to me as a child. He left home and started to train to be a solicitor, which is how he met Liz, a strait-laced young woman whose family called her 'Jane' (which meant they had to be posh; her sister also had a nickname, Mouse). They came from Hertfordshire – 'Terrible county' my dad would say. We all went to their wedding and my mum was bought her first outfit in 20 years: a brown shift and coat dress from Harrods. My dad was in morning dress, looking like Errol Flynn. I wore a petrol blue skirt and a too-tight, patterned shirt from Chelsea Girl tucked in. My hair was by now past my waist: I'd grown it to cover up my little seeds (I wouldn't say buds) of breasts. In the one and only photo of me I'm carrying a brown plastic clutch, which I have clamped over my stomach, convinced it stuck out obscenely. Clare is in a rust linen coat dress with a small waist, Lyn has a floppy picture hat over her long Cher hair, having arrived with her boyfriend Adrian, a doctor who drove a sports car and lived in Clapham.

All my brothers and sisters became more and more out of control. Not me, of course. I merely sewed daisy patches on my jeans and stole my sisters' cow bells to string around my neck over my green-and-red-stripe nylon polo neck from Chelsea Girl.

Not long after Lyn moved out, a gypsy woman selling pegs and tea towels came to our great, big, green front door with its stained-glass windows (when we went to Mrs Manders', my mum had to take our enormous door key; it weighed her down like an anchor). The gypsy told my mum that one of her daughters was being chased by demons and would live a very difficult life. My mum told me this at the time, which was odd, given she usually tried to protect me, her little girl, from all dangers, real or imagined. My mum was, indeed, so protective that she never expected anything of me other than surviving to adulthood without getting run over. It was sort of understandable, given the A130 at the bottom of our lane (we called the family who lived on the other side of the lane 'the gyppos'; even then I worried about Peg, a border collie, chained to a kennel for years at a time), but mostly irrational, since her fear of me crossing roads continued into my forties.

Chapter two

THE FLORAL NEEDLECORD YEARS

I was afraid of everything. My first day at primary school, just turned six years old, I hadn't wanted to let go of my mum's hand and venture across the playground. The next day, the same thing happened. Each time she had to take me in. Finally, my mum persuaded me to run in alone and I was knocked over by a great big boy. You see? The worst does happen. All through my childhood, I was convinced my dad was going to crash his car on the way home from the Wheatsheaf, where he would go for a nightly Gin and It. I would lie in my narrow divan waiting to hear his Hillman Minx, which he always had to double declutch, crunch on the drive. Only then could I sleep. I was afraid of ghosts, too. Once, lying awake to wait for Dad, I heard someone hoeing the drive, even though it was dark and we were all in bed. I told my mum the next day. 'That was useful of them,' was all she said.

I was full of rage, as well. I wanted a real pony, not a rocking horse. For my ninth birthday my dad gave me a hobby horse. Not a hobby horse with a horse's head, although that would have been bad enough, but at least I'd have been able to pretend to canter about on it, instead of using poor old Pompey, but a hobby horse with a Yogi Bear head. I used it as a punching bag. Eventually my parents arranged for me to have riding lessons but I wasn't grateful for them, either. Instead, I was disappointed that I never woke up on my birthday to find a pony with a white blaze on his face grazing on the rough part of the lawn. Nothing was ever good enough for me. I asked my dad for 'My Sweet Lord' by George Harrison; what he got me was the *Top of the Pops* version, sung by someone else. It was cheaper. He didn't think I would notice or care. I never listened to it. It wasn't George. The same thing happened when my dad gave me a string of pearls for my birthday as a teenager. Years later, broke and living in London, I took them to a pawn shop. 'They're plastic,' the man said, pushing them back under the partition. 'No,' I said. 'That can't be right. My dad gave them to me.' The man just raised an eyebrow, as if to say, 'That's men for you.' I wanted my dad to take Penny the rabbit to the vet to have her claws trimmed. He baulked at the expense and said he would do it himself. I was to hold her back paws. But she was a big, strong, bad-tempered white rabbit and, as my dad closed the pliers, she struggled and I had to let go. The claw remained in the dreadful apparatus and Penny was left, hopping lopsidedly, slowly, now covered in blood. He had pulled the whole thing out, like a pedal tooth. I never forgave him. 'Why is he so mean?' I asked my mum, but she never asked him for anything. He was beyond reproach.

Primary school was hell. It meant I had to leave mummy-ness and the telly, and interact with children my own age. Given the horror of my profile in the dressing table, I was determined no one would see me from the side, so I kept turning, oddly, when someone spoke to me. I always wore handmade, hand-knitted clothes, while all the other girls had Ladybird. I could already read before I got there and was given the job of teaching others to do it, too. Sue was a couple of years above me. When I arrived, a teacher said to her, 'Your sister will soon knock the spots off you.' I didn't know what on earth she meant. Sue did. I was frightened of the teachers, especially the headmaster. I was afraid of the outdoor pool, the cold, the playground, the playing fields, the gym.

Clare, Philip, Nick and Lyn, and even Tony, were living adult lives, which just left me and Sue. I was terrified of my brothers and sisters, but of Sue most of all. She had failed the 11-plus and was at Beauchamp Secondary Modern. Now that we were at separate schools, I didn't have to endure her during the day but it made it worse when we got home. I would arrive back from primary school earlier than she did and one afternoon I borrowed her red cable-knit sweater, but then quickly put it back in her drawer when I saw her walking up the gravel drive. As soon as she got home, she felt it and discovered it was still warm. She threw it at me, ranting and raging. She found new and different ways to torment me. She skipped her homework. One assignment was to review a book, which she never bothered to read; that night, she asked me to tell her what the story was about. I talked for hours and only in the morning did she tell me that she had fallen asleep almost at once, and hadn't heard a word.

As we were the two youngest, we were usually lumped together. We were always, and probably still are, 'the two little girls'. While Sue's socks crumpled round her ankles, mine were pulled taut to my scabby knees, secured with a rubber band. We were frogmarched to visit relatives. I hated going to stay with Granny Jones in London. While my mum would give you the food out of her own mouth and I don't think was ever left a suet dumpling once she'd doled out her famous stew, Granny Jones was mean. She took me and Sue to London Zoo once, my first ever trip on a train, and the thought of the stringy ham sandwiches she gave us to eat in the car park still makes me gag (throughout my entire childhood eating out involved being in a car in a car park somewhere; I didn't go inside a restaurant until I was 15 – there were simply too many of us, it would have been an invasion, and far too expensive). I remember she had a choc ice but wouldn't share it. She made me and my sister do embroidery in the evenings, then told me off for all the knots on the back of my piece of card. I couldn't knit, either: the needles would become rigid, an impenetrable tepee, within minutes. An early sign of stress. I put tiny pearls from my bead swap box in her sugar dispenser in the hope they would kill her. My sister Sue, the other half of the little girl double act, the person whose still-warm, pilled clothes I had to wear, made her first physical attack on me during an imprisonment at Granny Jones's. The old bat put us in a double bed. That night, Sue kicked me. All night. I don't know if she meant to and, if she did, I have no idea why. I didn't defend myself. Looking back, I wonder I didn't jump out of bed and go running screaming into Granny's room, or tell my mum when we got back home. I suppose I was too scared. I assumed this was to be my fate.

The girls from the housing estate across the A130 were my only friends: there was Gillian Neville, who was my best friend and a bit fat; and Penny Cresswell, a small, timid girl with guinea pigs in her back garden. There were no parties, no goodie bags, no pretty pink frothy dresses. Just pinafores. I was invited out, once. On a Sunday morning, Penny Cresswell came up the big stone steps to our green front door and knocked on the much-polished knocker.

'Would you like to go to the zoo?'

'Oh. Okay. Thanks,' I said, and shut the door.

I went inside and played with Yogi Bear for a bit, punching him, and Mum called me in for lunch. There was roast with Yorkshires, and apple pie with 'top of the milk'. Then there was another knock on the front door. I went and opened it, trying to hold Pompey back, who was barking. On the steps were Penny and her mum and dad, who were both very red in the face.

'We have been waiting in The Chase for two hours,' said Mr Cresswell.

I hadn't realised they'd meant now. I'd never been invited anywhere before and they never invited me again.

While Mum was always too busy operating the mangle and making tinned mandarin orange sponge tarts to ever take me on an outing (school trips to London Zoo and St Paul's, where I didn't have the shilling to go up in the tower so had to stay on my own in the pews, were the only time I ever went anywhere vaguely interesting), my brothers and sisters never suggested we do anything together, like go to a film or to a park, either. No one even offered to help me cross the main road at the bottom of our lane so I was stranded in the big, cold house (we had to scratch the ice off the inside of the windows in the morning, and my flannel always froze in its place by the sink. I thought everyone had red, mottled inner thighs, due to the fact they were clamped round a hot water bottle each night) on the north side of the A130, next to the church with its yew tree and beds of nettles. Living there was like being a permanent spectator at a Formula 1 race, the whine of the cars a backdrop to my barren, boring life.

I was ashamed to bring my friends from primary school home to play. The green paint was peeling on the outside of all our windows and the brown three-piece suite was threadbare. I much preferred their little boxy council houses with fitted carpets and ornaments. I was ashamed of my mum, too, which is an awful thing to say: she was so old, so handmade, not blonde and glamorous and young and kitten heeled, like my friends' mums. I wanted everything to be perfect and, until it was, until I was ready, I would rather I was left alone and no one saw the imperfections. Such was the chaos around me – the washing up, the arguments, the fact we were squished round the dining table for 11 months of the year to save coal, the queues for the cold bathroom, my hand-knitted jumpers, the skirts with liberty bodices attached, the one pair of shoes, the half a house, the wobbly eggs – I always felt things, life, surroundings but, mainly, me could be improved. One day they would be, I thought, so let's wait until then to invite anyone round. This feeling of not being ready for inspection continued all through my life: I'd have a man coming round to dinner and I would mow the lawn (actually, no, I didn't do that: I had it returfed), power hose the wheelie bin, buy a new sofa, wax and jog and pluck and tan myself, and only then would I be ready.

Gillian came a few times after school, though, for weak squash (we had fizzy drinks at Christmas when Mum bought 'bombs' from Bonds for the green soda siphon: thank goodness this was an age before Islamic terrorism). Once, we played up on the now-empty top floor (I used to roller skate on the floorboards: 'Is it thunder?' my mum would ask), and Gill pulled down her pants to show me her first strands of pubic hair, aged ten. I was shocked, and revolted. Why was that happening to her? Would it happen to me, too? How disgusting! She was a day younger than me and nothing like that was happening to me so far. I was as hairless down there as

Sindy. Most important of all, though, was how could I stop it?

I started to lie about this time, too; a habit that would become a lifetime one. I told the girls in the council estate that we owned the whole house, not half of it, which was fine until one of them saw Mrs Little at a window and asked who on earth she was. (I always hated the Littles. The family kept their Labradors chained to kennels outside. There was one, a flea-bitten, cream-coloured bitch, whose eyes always watered terribly in the sun, but they never brought her indoors. The father used to whip her, too. I thought that was terrible. Even when Pompey bit my dad so badly the white bones on his knuckles showed through the wound, he just said, 'Oh, he didn't mean it, Mummy.' My dad kissed the dog repeatedly, which he never did with me, this from an old-fashioned man with the army's brusqueness and upright decorum who had no truck with emotions and frailty.)

I wanted a pony so much, I pretended I had one. The Littles' daughter had a grey pony called Puck and I was incredibly jealous. 'What is your pony called?' Penny asked me. Caught unawares, I replied, 'Fuck.'

She looked shocked, and then she giggled and covered her mouth.

'What, don't you believe me?' I said.

'No, it's just . . . Don't you know what that means? Did your mum say you could name it that?'

I had no idea what it meant.

I was scared of the boys in my primary school, too,

although I had a crush on one, Stuart Watts, who lived in a house by the roundabout. He had an air of Eric Burdon of The Animals about him – skin slightly pock marked and the colour of an uncooked apple pie. He once gave me a Slinky: this is a spring that could walk down stairs. It soon became tangled and ruined, which was unfortunate as a week or so later he asked for it back. I'd walk to his house dragging Pompey, who would never go in the direction you wanted unless you bribed him with Tuc biscuits, and just stare up at his house. If he'd have come outside I'd have run away.

Then something happened that made me retreat from boys further. It was playtime. We were never allowed to stay indoors at playtime, even if it was snowing. But on this day it was so cold, we decided to play in the corridors. A group of boys pushed me into their loo – and I knew the boys' loos were off-limits and a terrible place. I'd smell it as I passed: a boy, urine smell. I knew it was dangerous and cold and slimy. The boys pushed me down on the ground – one was called Richard. I was giggling, from sheer nerves, and then I was screaming. They lifted up my scratchy jumper and saw above my red plaid skirt was sewn a sort of white nylon vest: my mum didn't believe in little girls having skirts with waist-bands, she thought they hung better from a bodice. The boys found this garment extremely hilarious. I frantically pulled my woolly down. Where were the other girls? Why were they not helping me? I remember shouting 'Penny!' as Richard dug his fingers into my hairless vagina. I never told anyone, never breathed a word.

I learned then that boys are not human. These ones certainly weren't (I didn't have a male friend until 1989, when I developed a relationship with a gay colleague, and I haven't had another one since). They are not to be trusted. They will humiliate you and take what they want. They will laugh at you. I didn't even tell my mum what had happened, so ashamed was I. And it would have been easy to do, as she was right there outside, by then 'earning a few bob' as a dinner lady: the only paid employment she ever had. It meant I could no longer escape school and go home for lunch to watch *The Woodentops* and *The Flower Pot Men* (the mythical, looming presence of the gardener always had me terrified). Mum would limp around the playground, herding strays in her bouclé wool, second-hand coat, banana sandwiches in her pocket, which she would hand to me furtively, slightly squashed and warm, for my lunch as we could never afford proper school dinners.

I was aware we were struggling. My mum ran up a £60 bill at Thompson's, a grocer's a short bus ride away, and she was terrified my dad would find out. She wasn't scared of him, that wasn't it. She hadn't bought perfume or stockings, merely food. I think she just wanted to do her best; it was in her nature to cope. She never once asked Dad not to go to the pub, or not to buy a new shirt, so why was she so secretive about this debt?

I never had any new clothes that weren't handmade, not really, apart from a teddy bear anorak from Bonds that only managed to make me look bulky. Once when we went to

Bonds, Sue and I were told we could choose any fabric we liked. I chose blue needlecord covered in flowers; Sue chose red needlecord. My mum ran us up super-trendy dresses with long sleeves and zips up the front. Because I always had to wear Sue's hand-me-downs, I was destined to be in floral needlecord for the next five years.

I remember when I modelled the teddy bear anorak in front of Lyn, her saying, 'You look straight out of Carnaby Street!' Wow! Do I? What on earth does that mean? I didn't have a clue – I'd get on Lyn's nerves every night, asking, after lights out, as she crept past our door to go upstairs, 'What can I think about?' And so she bought me a Beatles magazine at the station, and gave me a photo of Paul McCartney in a field surrounded by daisies to pin on my wardrobe in the room I shared with Sue. After Davy Jones, it was the second time I fell in love. When the Beatles' live appearance at Shea Stadium was on the telly, I said to Lynnie, 'I watched the entire concert without blinking once!'

'Don't be stupid,' she'd said. 'That's not possible.'

I only remember the slights, the barbs, however small. When Sue asked Lyn who was better looking, her or me (Sue, with fair, curly hair resembled a young Dora Bryan, while I was in my Batgirl phase, wearing a black velvet cape around my shoulders), Lyn replied, 'Sue is pretty, Lizzie is handsome.' I reeled. I'm that boy again, the man in the moon.

Every morning, Mum would bring me toast and marmalade and coffee (Gold Blend instant; ordinary Nescafé, like ITV, was considered common) in bed. I was sitting up, taking delivery of this on a Saturday, aged 11, when Sue, in the single divan across the room, said, 'You'll get fat if you eat that.'

'Really?'

'There are loads of calories in that toast. And in orange juice. And a can of tuna.'

My mum, shuffling around the room, opening curtains and collecting laundry, did not tell Sue off for saying this to me. If she had said anything, it would have been, 'A little won't hurt' or 'You must eat something.'

I was due to go for a riding lesson that morning (I went once a week, my black cap, the only proper 'kit' I owned, would be carefully wrapped in cellophane between each outing; I still recall the delicious smell of new velvet) and I told Sue that, if I didn't eat, I would probably fall off Flicka, the black pony with the sensitive withers. But, as I propped on one elbow and chewed and sipped, I thought about what I was eating for the very first time. The butter must have been hard, so it was in big lumps on the toast. The marmalade – home-made, of course, in a great, big, steel pan – had large bits of peel that I always picked out and placed around the side. And I have never stopped thinking about food to this day: what I ate today and what I will eat tomorrow.

At last I had a purpose to my day, and I would be better at it than any of my sisters had been. I would be on a diet, and I would be good at being on a diet. I would be unswerving in my commitment and my application. I would have a grilled tom and maybe an egg. Never a Yorkshire. Nothing swimming with fat – spitting, hot, greasy. It was as though a switch had been turned in my head – and many other sufferers from eating disorders have told me it also just took one unkind word, or a photo, for their switch to be clicked. From then on, I felt that flesh was bad and lazy. Flesh caused problems and mess and expense: bleeding and towels and boys and gunshot weddings and arguments and overdoses and tears. And it meant I wasn't trying hard enough to be good.

Within months, when I turned up at the office of the riding school, in a village called Stock, the owner, a hard-faced woman, looked in her book to tell me the name of the pony I had been assigned and, as she glanced up at me, told me she was worried I was getting so thin. She didn't tell my dad, who was sitting, patiently, in his car waiting for me (like most children, I wasn't grateful my dad spent a good part of his Saturday driving me around, and waiting). But I loved the feeling that being thin, almost weightless, gave me. I was good at it. I would gaze, not at my face, but at my jutting collar-bone in the mirror, run my fingers across my ribs like a xylophone player. I wanted to look as small as I felt.

My reading matter was a curious, heady mix. Of my sisters' magazines and the second-hand pony books my mum snuffled out for me at jumble sales (*A Stable for Jill*, *Jill Has Two Ponies*, *Jill's Pony Trek*: you get the idea, there was always another child's name pencilled in the first page), my favourite was *Riders from Afar*, by a Pullein-Thompson sister. It describes how two large American children come to

England in the Fifties to rent a castle from an aristocratic but cash-strapped family. I imagined I was the dark and petite Right Honourable Chloe. I still have this copy, marked 2/6d, and I have inserted into the title with blue Biro – not just now, way back then – an 'f' and an 'i', forming the word 'affair'. Just because I didn't understand why Guinea the guinea pig and Penny the rabbit, both female and different species, weren't making children in their hutch didn't mean I had no need for romance. I remember reading the Famous Five, too, and being puzzled in the one where they meet people from a circus and Julian says a snake is as big as his calf. 'When did he get a baby cow?' I wondered, flicking back through the pages for something I must have missed. I also took delivery of a weekly comic called *Diana* until it became too expensive (Sue had, instead, *Beryl the Peril*, whose father used to take her over his knee and spank her with a slipper). *Diana* was not all pink and girly, as these magazines are today, but instead had plucky girls on ponies on the cover, jumping coloured poles. Its heroines would go fishing, play the violin, dive, ski and toboggan or find a lost sheep, or even clean their parents' car. (I often, while still in primary school, did Bob-a-Job, which involved knocking on neighbours' houses and doing anything they asked for money. Oddly, this was not considered dangerous.) I still have the February 1965 issue of *Diana*: a hatless girl on a horse, galloping on a beach, and inside a free fake diamond ring. I didn't wear the ring but wrapped it in tissue and hid it inside my velvet riding cap.

And later, aged 11, I borrowed Sue's *Jackie*. There were no photos in *Jackie* in the late Sixties, or ponies, just psychedelic drawings of very long-limbed girls with swirly hair and huge eyes whose only pursuit was boys.

My mum never, ever talked to me about boys, or sex, or growing up. I didn't want to become a nurse or a housewife – blood scared me, cuddles scared me, real men scared me, including my dad, my dolls scared me, so I'm sure babies would too – but no other option had ever been spoken of. I overheard her once asking Lyn to get Sue a deodorant, to leave it in her room on her chest of drawers. My mum never had the housekeeping money to buy anything remotely frivolous and, as Lyn was now earning, she thought she could help out. I imagine Sue was starting to smell. I knew girls wore bras, as I'd seen Lyn in hers, but I had no idea why, or where to get hold of one. In primary school, some of the girls aged ten, such as Hazel, who lived in a smart bungalow with a willow tree in the garden and a stuffed badger indoors, were growing breasts and wearing bras. I crept into my mum's room and took out her suspenders and girdle: they were made of blue-and-white gingham. I fashioned them into a bra. A few girls at school were saying that when we got bigger we would lay eggs and bleed. 'That can't be right,' I said. 'That is disgusting.' At no point had it ever crossed my mind to wonder how babies were made, or what would happen when Paul McCartney eventually turned up and asked me to marry him.

*

The only thing I learned as a child, quite thoroughly, was how to fail; at least I always felt I was failing, somehow. Not just how not to come first, but how not to even be awarded a Highly Commended. This was done via the torture of the Horticultural Show, held on the cricket field behind the Town Hall, next to Mrs Manders'. Every year, I entered various classes. I was the only member of my family who ever entered these competitions. I wanted to do well, but was never quite good enough. But it would be an action echoed years later when I put my head above the precipice and took the job as editor of *Marie Claire* magazine, against my better judgement. I was an early proponent, therefore, of the philosophy of Feel the Fear and Do It Anyway. For the painting competition, I decided to do a collage of Pompey, using his fur, collected in a comb. The comment next to my entry stated, 'Smells, and I suspect has fleas.'

I entered 'Garden in a Saucer'. I had no template, no idea what I needed to live up to. I got my chipped saucer – willow-pattern, of course – and covered it with earth, a few pebbles and tiny daisies picked from the lawn and which soon wilted due to lack of moisture. On the way to the marquee, buffeted by the traffic on the A130, I tripped and landed on the saucer. I scraped it all back together. It was now a saucer of dirt. My mum, though, who never criticised me or told me something was not good enough, said it was 'Very good, Darling.'

Imagine my horror when I got inside the tent, with its smell of warm grass, to a sea of miniature paradises: teeny mirrors for ponds, teeny swings and puppies playing, mini flowers and turf, paths made from jewels. I placed my saucer, thankfully soon to be anonymous, on the edge of the trestle, where a great big man used it as an ashtray.

There was 'Dress the Wooden Spoon', too, and I had high hopes for this one. I had dressed my spoon in my Sindy's riding outfit, which I felt really suited it. Other girls, though, had done differently: hand-knitted sweaters, sequined skating skirts, velvet capes and bell-bottom trousers. One spoon was even a ballerina, with handmade tiny ballet shoes in pink leather and a teeny tiara. My equestrian Sindy was duly ignored. It was largely felt I'd cheated. I dreamed of being like the plucky girls on the cover of *Diana*, but I just did not have the wherewithal in reality. One summer, my Aunt Ethel, married to Uncle Les, a brittle woman, felt sorry for me and my series of failures and, as a teacher, decided to take me in hand. She painted a portrait of the Mona Lisa on the side of a huge cardboard box, cut out the face, and put me inside for the 'Fancy Dress'. She glued an old picture frame around the periphery. I remember walking in a circle behind all the cowboys and Indians, the princesses and the fairies. My box smelled of Bovril crisps. But it had not contained crisps, as I found out to my dismay and shame, as bigger girls started to titter. Words seeped through the watercolour wash on the back of the box. It had contained sanitary towels. The sort of sanitary towels that had stirrups you would loop round a waist belt. I had no idea what these items were, of course, or what they were for. But there I was on display – a giant sanitary towel.

Chapter three

'PLEASE EXCUSE LIZZIE, SHE HAS A PERSISTENT VERRUCA'

I'm in a tiny wooden changing room. The floor is wet, which is dangerous – I could fall over and crack my skull. As it is, I'm frozen and keep knocking my elbows. I'm in my black regulation costume, trying to get my thick head of hair into my swimming cap. My cap is not like the other girls', who have plain cream or black sporty ones. Mine is covered in giant flowers. My mum said her cap would do. I tried pulling a flower off, which resulted in a small hole. I also have Pompey's pale green towel, as there wasn't another one spare. Unlike me, it's bald.

I emerge, wrapped in the doggy towel. Miss Goodwin, my form mistress, who has only a claw for a hand (she rescued someone from a burning building during the Blitz, but this matters little to me, aged 11: it's a claw and I don't want to be in its vice-like grip), blows her whistle. She is always doing this. What about just indicating by pointing that I should get in the cold, slimy water, which actually has frogs and newts? I have so much hair in the cap, my head looks like the Elephant Man's. Sarah Trembling, the most beautiful girl in Form 3B at Brentwood County High, is already powering up and down, performing the butterfly stroke, a feat as impossible to me as all the members of Showaddywaddy turning up to pick me up after school.

I sit on the side, dipping my toes in the water. I'm still attached to the towel, like Linus. This is hell. I am near naked, I am freezing, and I am going to have to be athletic and sporty. Miss Goodwin tugs the towel from beneath my dappled thighs. 'What was your mother thinking, sending you with this? It's no more good than a napkin!'

I place my feet on the metal steps. All around me girls with coltish limbs jump or dive in. How did they learn to do that? The shock of the water around my midriff makes me gasp. Someone splashes me. Don't do that. I'm in. Oh no, my feet don't touch the bottom. I panic and grab the sides. Miss Goodwin hands me a white square polystyrene float. I hug it to my chest, for all the world as if shipwrecked, and kick out behind. I have churning bubbles in my wake, while the other girls leave a mere slipstream. Sarah Trembling powers past me. Karen Rouse, a Karen Carpenter lookalike, is performing backstroke, barely making a ripple. Barbara Fielding, or Babs, with bright blue eyes and black curls, a female David Essex, is doing the breaststroke. While I'm a human stone. I don't even move from my spot. Perhaps my hair, partially escaping from its flowery bower and now like seaweed, is holding me back. This is pointless. I have a swimming headache.

When my dad opened my 11-plus results, we were in the tiny galley kitchen dodging flies. 'You have failed miserably!' he said.

Oh no. Oh, well. It's to be expected. Nothing I do ever works out. Perhaps this is what the Horticultural Show was all about: preparing me for future blows.

'Only joking! You passed with flying colours!'

No one hugged me. My mum said 'Well done, Darling', while Sue glowered, in her red cable-knit sweater.

The high school my parents chose for me was miles away in Brentwood, which is practically in Romford. I would get a lift with my dad in the morning, whose blood transfusion office was in Shenfield nearby, but after school there would be the Long Trek Home. A walk or, more often, a run, clutching my wicker basket to my blazer, from the school to the station, then a train to Wickford ('Always get in a through carriage', my mum would say. 'Not the single, separate ones, because a Man Could Get In'), then a bus, after a long wait, and then a walk up the steep hill from the Turnpike roundabout. I think if this journey were to happen today, it would be classified as abuse. Sometimes I'd ring the changes and get off at Rayleigh station, then catch the number 11 bus. It took longer, but avoided the uphill walk.

My parents chose Brentwood County High School so that I could get that lift in the morning, not really thinking through the hours it would take me to crawl home. I was bought my first uniform at Bonds, of course: a navy skirt (we had to kneel on the playground to prove to the teachers it was the correct length – if it didn't become brushed with hop-scotch chalk we were for it), blue-and-white-checked blouse, and a navy blazer. Except we couldn't afford the blazer. There was a hat, too, and a navy raincoat, but we couldn't afford those either. There were navy culottes for hockey, hockey boots and plimsolls, and a white Aertex blouse, which I am pretty certain, along with the rest of my 'PE kit', only got washed once a year. But my dad and I bonded on those hour-long drives in the Hillman Minx, with 'Chirpy Chirpy Cheep Cheep' on the radio. He would give me two bob to buy sweets on the way home, which I saved up to buy myself jodhpurs.

There were three grammar schools in Brentwood in those days: the Ursuline, with a brown uniform, for Catholic girls; Brentwood School for boys, nicknamed Bugs, where Nick had gone; and us. We all hated each other.

Even aged 11 I was very aware of the architecture of the school and what I liked and didn't like. I liked the old, bay-windowed front of the building, and the wooden parquet floor outside the office of the headmistress, Miss Rayner. (She later, exciting much scandal, became Mrs Lansdell, having married one of the builders who were erecting prefabs and concreting over the hockey field when the school 'turned comp': this meant younger boys would soon be in our midst! There was much excitement when we older girls thought we'd see boys every day, but they were all weedy, with Dave Hill haircuts, like mini versions of the members of Slade, but doubly ugly.) I liked the quad and the corridors paved with stone, and the wood-panelled library. I liked the ancient hut where the hockey sticks were stored. But I hated the slimy, unheated pool and, eventually, the modern sports hall with bars up the side (these bars were never used. I always wondered what they were for. I used to hang my socks on them to air).

I was not like the other girls at BCHS. We had a great, big, smelly loo just off the quad and it had a mirror. I didn't want to look in this mirror, for obvious reasons, and so developed a technique of sliding along one wall towards the wash basins and standing to one side, never looking up. Slide and never look up. It's a technique that has served me well to this day. Don't do it, don't meet your own eyes. It has made any sort of conversation with my hairdresser and colourist these days a little hard, as I always twist in my chair to look at him. If I meet my own eyes in the mirror I will be turned to stone, like the goldfish in the *Singing Ringing Tree*.

And then, one Christmas, having saved her dinner lady money, my mum bought me a No7 box set of make-up. In it was a green tube of very brown foundation, a mascara and a lipstick! I put the foundation on, using my fingers, and found I was able to look at just half of my face in the mirror (not the whole face, just a glimpse, a segment, a postage

71

stamp square). It was a miracle! I added green Mary Quant eye shadow and green Mary Quant nail polish: the shade was Moss. My brothers said I looked partly decayed. It wasn't vanity, though, it was a mask. I had started paying more attention to what I was wearing, as well, and discovered Freeman, Hardy & Willis on Brentwood High Street. For £3.75 (we now 'have decimals', as Mrs Manders would say – I think it was decimals that finally killed her off) I bought a pair of brown rubber platforms. They can be seen, momentarily discarded, in the picture of me, fully dressed in jeans and blue towelling top, on the 'beach' – really, a strip of hard pebbles – in Jersey. Earlier that day, I had applied Jolen Creme Bleach to my upper lip and upper thighs, which caused much knocking on the door of the shared-by-many bathroom of the Fawlty Towersesque hotel. I'd had to scrape off the pungent cream prematurely, hence the denim cover-up. Frances Gibb, a girl from my class, came with us, at a cost to her mum of £75, and complained bitterly throughout about the weather, the lack of discos, the ancient device on the wall of our bedroom that refused to accept the Radio 1 Roadshow. I was quite pleased at the wind and rain, as I was worried about premature ageing. I was 13 years old.

But, even in uniform, I managed to look as hideous as I had in my formative, brown-velvet-hot-panted years. On the long sprint to catch the train every night, I would twist my ankle frequently in my one and only pair of platforms, and knock the ankle bone, causing great big red scabs. I think my body was making a half-hearted attempt at puberty by this stage, fuelled by a diet that consisted solely of brown bread and banana sandwiches with NO butter, because butter makes you fat, and is off the *19* magazine calorie counter scale. Puberty manifested itself not by making me shapely or tall, but by producing copious amounts of sebum on my scalp. I had very long hair, grown to cover my body at all times, like fur, but also, perversely given the grease which you'd have thought would have made its way down to the tips to moisturise them, split ends. They showed up very white against my dark hair, like perilously low-slung dandruff, and on Saturdays I would embark on the pilgrimage to Chelmsford to visit the Mecca that was Boots, in order to buy Protein 21. It came in a reassuringly pharmaceutical white bottle, was covered in small print, and it promised to mend split ends. What a lie! I was thus simultaneously both greasy and dry. School geography field trips, which involved a coach ride to go to look at truncated spurs somewhere outside Maldon, made me queasy, as I didn't want anyone to sit behind me and see my split ends and wonder at the grease on my scalp. I don't know why my mum didn't just cut the ends off. But, again, I was left not to take this time, but to go to seed and fester.

By the lower IVth, Sue had joined my school, as she'd taken the 13-plus. We never really interacted, though. Once, Sue and her older friends stood behind me in assembly. On the long walk home together later that day, Sue told me that, 'You might have the longest hair in school, but it's also the greasiest.'

She was friends with the beautiful Nicole who had no split ends and wanted to be a doctor. You see, there were girls around me with ambition, but I never had any. I was hopeless at all the sciences and terrible at art. I hated the blue overalls: my only achievement was to fashion a Ronald Biggs puppet out of papier mâché. He had a very pink face and a curly, black and not-true-to-life-at-all afro, as I'd made his hair by cutting up my mum's second-hand astrakhan cape; there was no reprimand.

Some of the girls, including Sarah Trembling (Trembling by name, Trembling by nature! She had a bra and a boyfriend), were 'getting their period'. This was something they were all rather smug and proud about. They couldn't go swimming because they were 'getting their period'. I never got mine – there was a scant brown stain circa 1973 — so, in order to avoid going in the frog-spawn-infested pool, I had to get my mum to write a heartfelt letter to Miss Goodwin saying, 'Please excuse Lizzie, she has a very persistent verruca that we're finding hard to shift.' Oh, the shame, the lack of glamour. And while they all trooped into Woolworths to buy 'tow-els' along with their sweets, I never had to. I didn't need towels and I never bought sweets, ever since the marmalade debacle when I had got myself a calorie counter in Boots and discovered how many calories there were in a ban, a slice of toast, an apple. I wasn't going to risk sweets. I wanted to wear a towel very badly, though. But I was scared of them, too. I'd smell them in the girls' loo: a horrid, dried blood smell. I didn't ever want to smell like that. I was once given detention for giggling in class and my punishment was to write notices for each toilet cubicle in the school: Please place your sanitary towel in the bin. When my mum asked me what I'd had to write, I couldn't tell her.

Because I was never getting my period, I had to contort my body in all sorts of dreadful sport, day in, day out. Gymnastics. What use is this discipline in everyday life? I had to wear navy knickers and the Aertex blouse. We had rush mats but, even so, I found a forward roll painful and difficult. When it came to climbing the rope, I never got off the ground. I just dipped and swung, like a silent campanologist. The other girls, the Karens and the Sarahs and the Melanies and the Christines, would be vaulting over the horse, but I would always refuse, just as my feet were about to lift off the floor. No, I can't do it. Hurdling and high jump? I would baulk, or run out, like a donkey at the Grand National, courage failing me. In hockey, I was repeatedly hit by a stick on my already-assaulted ankle bones. Rounders involved arguments about who was in and who was out. I took Country Dancing, which involved Miss Goodwin gripping my shoulders, once again. In a rare show of confidence, I choreographed four friends in the BCHS talent contest in a sort of Pan's People homage, to the strains of 'Sweet Talking Guy' and 10cc's 'I'm Not in Love' (the line 'Don't you forget' was acted by the girls pointing at their brains, then waggling their fingers). We'd rehearse in my garage, trying not to trip over Penny the rabbit, who had been temporarily allowed to taste freedom. We came third.

I wanted to be thin, like the girls in *Honey* and *Jackie* and *19* (oh, how I loved Sue's *19* magazine, with its dreamy covers, and beauty tips ... I'd spend hours poring over diagrams of how to shade and highlight my cheekbones), but I didn't want to expose my figure by exercising it. I fell in love with the body of Olga Korbut. She was my ideal, like a ten-year-old child. I can picture her to this day: pigtails, a crumpled face, that bony sternum, the perfect S-bend her childlike body made as she hovered and teetered on the bar, like a pipe cleaner, or flung herself backwards from the parallel bars, only to land in tears. No boy fancied Olga Korbut, but I loved her.

Other than double gym, the day I dreaded above all others was 'Wear your own clothes Friday'. This was to raise money for charity, an early precursor to Live Aid, Comic Relief, et al. But I didn't really have my own clothes, not now we'd invested in the uniform. All I had was a bright yellow blouse with gypsy sleeves, a pair of flared brown loons with a broken zip, as I had lain on the candlewick bedspread once too often pulling them up with a coat hanger, and my rubbery brown FHW platforms (I never did have the prescribed 'indoor' and 'outdoor' shoes). That was it. So each time we collected money for the poor, I had to wheel out the same old outfit. It was humiliating. While the other girls were in red velvet smocks and tartan kilts and tartan dresses with white frilly bibs and white patterned tights and fab gold chain belts, I was in the loons that smelled of kitchen, since I had a Sunday job washing up in the Wheatsheaf to help pay for riding lessons.

I hated that job. I was by now vegetarian, having been frightened by Granny's stories of slaughtering the pig, and then having seen the cartoon of *Animal Farm* on TV, taking it rather literally, so couldn't stand the greasy swill in each pan I washed up. This Wheatsheaf experience put me off eating out for life: there was a cold room across the alleyway containing the smelly bins and inside were Black Forest gateaux and rum babas covered in mouse droppings that the randy French waiter, Michel, who reminded me of Roberto Rivelino, who played for Brazil in the 1970 World Cup, would scrape off (a black bristly moustache still makes me blush – oh, tie a yellow ribbon round me any day). In the end, I refused to wash up any plate that had had meat on it, so I was relegated to the children's bar at the end of the garden. I'd stand behind the tiny wooden trestle table, with my Tizers and cream sodas and R Whites lemonade, waiting for teeny customers who never came. I never sold a single item. As I was on commission, I never got paid.

At school, I was excused Biology as I refused to dissect a bull's eye. I couldn't do Maths, and could only play the first bar of 'Good King Wenceslas' on the recorder: the spit disgusted me. I attended Needlework, but it took me four years to complete a basic nightie. In Domestic Science, I only got as far as 'cheesy potatoes'.

Add to all these shortcomings the fact I needed braces: my teeth crossed over at the front, even the bottom ones. The first time the dentist put the braces on, I actually fainted – they were cemented to my teeth, top and bottom, with a supply of teeny rubber bands to loop round the hooks on the wire. My mum, who was with me, said, 'You'll be glad we did this when you are older and go out with boys.' That was the first and last conversation we ever had about sex. (No, she did say just one other thing. On my wedding day, installed in her loft room at Babington House in Somerset, she said, after much rustling and rummaging and finally emerging triumphant from her ancient bag with a small Tupperware with a mismatched lid held in place with a rubber band, 'I've brought my own Rich Teas. You don't want to embark on married life in debt.')

The boys from Brentwood School, whom we'd spy on the station platform on the way home, were just not interested in me. At the youth club, they would talk to Gillian Saunders, who was blonde, had perfect, Marie Osmond teeth, and represented the school at tennis (I was assigned the job of ball girl). She had the most handsome, dark-haired boyfriend in the world: Taffy. I once, to my immense surprise, got off with his friend, Mick Spellar, who had terrible, volcanic acne, at a party at Karen Rouse's semi-detached in Billericay. I was in a brown nylon top with an appliquéd pattern on the chest. We snogged in his Mini Cooper. He promised to call me to take me to see *Quadrophenia*. I gave him our number: Wickford 3086. I had sleepless nights, tossing and turning, remembering the taste of his mouth, like an ashtray washed with Coca-Cola. If anyone kissed on the telly, I became embarrassed, convinced my mum could tell. The big black phone in the hall remained silent for the next 30 years.

We went on a rare family holiday at this time: we drove – minus Clare (married) and Philip and Nick (too old) – for what seemed like days (the M5 was not yet complete), crowded into the Hillman Minx, double declutching the whole way, to Sidmouth in south Devon. We stopped off at every cathedral along the way to eat sandwiches wrapped in greaseproof paper. We stayed in a flat in an old Victorian house called Willoughby. It's still there. I wonder if it still smells of gas and fresh cream doughnuts. There was absolutely nothing to do in Sidmouth: no telly, no warm weather, and we couldn't afford to eat out. The one and only thing we did was sit and watch a brass band on the bandstand. Lyn left halfway through the week on the train to be interviewed to start her nursing training. My dad, always shirtless, would disappear each day to take one of his long clifftop walks: he told us he had a compulsion to push people off a great height, which discouraged any taggers along. 'This isn't like *Bonjour Tristesse*, or *Girl with Green Eyes*,' I remember thinking, slathering on the sunblock, refusing to remove my clothes. 'It's just boring and windy, PLUS I have to place all the rubber bands around my hooks every night.' Food became stuck in my braces. I wanted to be leggy, with honeyed, south of France limbs, but my legs were mottled and stunted. There must be more to life. When we got back, Dad and I collected Pompey from the kennels. 'He tried to whelp with one of the bitches,' the woman said, handing Dad the lead, the dog jumping up, smiling. 'What does whelp mean?' I asked. 'Bite,' my dad said.

But, I don't know, maybe I was lithe, like a colt. My best friend at primary school had been Lesley Stacey, who lived opposite Thompson's the grocer's. One summer, when I was ten, she invited me to go on holiday to Bude in Cornwall with her family. Her brother, Michael, who looked just like Donny Osmond, came, too, and her two older male cousins. On the beach, I was covering myself in a towel so no one would see me, performing that strange dance, like a reverse, inept striptease, putting my clothes back on, when Lesley's dad said to her cousin 'Oh, to be on the beach with Liz in ten years' time', and they all smirked. Really? Will I be attractive to boys in ten years' time? This really bothered me. I don't want them watching me behind a towel when I am older, fancying me! I knew it would never be true, anyway. Someone offered me a pastie from one of those cold, damp, concreted cafés, and I hid it in my knitted Indian bag with tassels.

I only remember the beautiful girls at my high school. Frances Gibb, who had come to Jersey with us and whose father died when she was ten, lived in Burnham-on-Crouch, and had shapely calves and breasts, and a pair of PVC lace-up boots. There was Georgia Gotley, who was posh and who got pregnant. Babs, despite her small size, managed to get pregnant too. Karen Rouse, though, was my best friend and my first girl crush. She had a wavy, dark, feather cut, and a perfect nose. I would say her only fault was thick ankles. When she got off the train at Billericay, she would run alongside the train on the platform, mouthing, 'I love you, Lilly', which I think meant me. But nothing ever happened between us: the story of my life. (I met up with her again in 2008. She is living on a small island off the coast of Hong Kong, having had three children. I asked her then whether she remembers our schooldays fondly. 'You and me were a bit apart from every-one else,' she said. 'There were the pretty girls, and the nerds, and then there was us: dark and brooding. And I remember the bullying was horrible.')

Karen soon became catnip to boys, the rough sort, the mods who hung out in Southend. We went to fairs in Billericay, both in handmade 'tonic' skirts ('Johnny Reggae' was on *Top of the Pops* and this shiny, green fabric was all the rage). Late night, smelly affairs (God knows why my mum and dad allowed this), we would walk to her house after-wards, she pursued by boys, me carrying our Crombies. I settled for being in love with Marc Bolan (whom I always assumed was black), David Cassidy and, finally, David Essex: it was distant adoration, the safe sort. My sisters went after real men. Mine were all two-dimensional. I was so shy I didn't even kiss my David Cassidy poster on the mouth and make him wet, like my friends did. I wouldn't even get into my vest and pants in front of his poster. Karen, Babs and I had got in to see David Essex in *That'll Be the Day*, which had an 18 cer-tificate. It scarred me for decades. The randiness. The hormones. He was all hands. It was a double bill with *Enter the Dragon*. I decided Bruce Lee was entirely my type: sinewy, dark skinned, other.

I only got one other snogging during my entire time in high school. It was the school dance in the library (all we are

81

missing is a piece of lead piping), and took place to the strains of 'All Right Now' by Free. A boy with Marc Bolan's hair kissed me (yes, sir, I can boogie). I never found out his name. I never saw him again. What can I say? It was a pattern. If only one of these boys had called me, perhaps my life would have been normal. There was a point when I was still whole: no scars, a working womb, a face yet to be lifted, blepharoplasty yet to be performed, breasts still as God made them, the thin, scant arc of an eyebrow from over-plucking to look like the girl in the Sara Moon poster. If the boy with Marc Bolan's hair had been more proactive, I would now own things like rolling pins. I would possess an oven that actually heats up, have giant teenage children and a greying husband asleep in a chair. I'd own a pair of tights, a bag of flour. Salt. Sugar. A tin of biscs.

My sister Sue, though, all brown, crinkled PVC midi coat over a hand-knitted, striped tank top, polka dot Laura Ashley maxi with ruffled hem, a piecrust blouse, feather-cut hair, livid blue eye shadow and a dire need for Quinoderm, had discovered boys. Namely Steve, a Peter Hammill lookalike (Sue had also discovered Van der Graaf Generator, of which Hammill was lead singer), all long, dark hair and sinews, skin that had never seen the sun. She first spotted him on the number 11 bus we'd catch home from Rayleigh station after school. He always sat on the top deck at the front, with his friend, whom we named, in a rather non-PC fashion, Blackie. He wore a donkey jacket. Our days and lives soon revolved around whether or not we would see Steve and Blackie on the bus. When our school was closed once, due to fleas, we walked Pompey down The Chase, just so we could see Steve's girly silhouette flash past. While we waited, a cat from the estate opposite started to cross the A130, spied Pompey at our heels, and hesitated, elegant paw poised in midair. In that split second the number 11 bowled into view and squashed the cat. But Sue got her glimpse of Steve.

I think all this was aversion therapy. Disaster will strike if Lizzie ever has fun, or bunks off, or does something frivolous. I was Sue's beard for several years after this incident because she and Steve eventually started going out. They'd meet in his home town of Chelmsford. Because Steve, barely 20, was married with a baby, my parents barred Sue from seeing him again: they only found out because his irate wife rang 3086. So I was taken along on these clandestine dates, she in a white Afghan coat, me in a hand-me-down brown one with orange embroidery, to endless rendezvous at the Odeon, then nights of the long swords at the bus garage as we waited for the sign at the front of the green bus to be hand-cranked from Chelmsford to Southend, so that we could go home at last.

One of the cinema outings was to see *Butch Cassidy and the Sundance Kid*. I was already in love with Paul Newman: *Hud* had initiated me into his moody blue stare, while *Sweet Bird of Youth* had ignited a yearning for pale denim. Each year Dad splashed out and bought the Christmas double issue of *Radio Times* and I would scour the listings for his name, then circle each entry with a swirl. I lived for films, any film: it was a couple of hours when I could forget about me. One Christmas, I watched 42 and wrote a small review of each in a notebook. Aged 11, I made a list of all the things I needed to make life complete, and it read:

Fab chain belt
White tights
Hardback biography of Paul Newman
Blue Wella conditioner sachet x 2
Proper jodhs this time, not stirrup pants

Sue stole my wish list and said, 'Biography of Paul Newman? You're mad! Why is that essential?' But to me, it was, like oxygen. And so, on that particular night I didn't much mind being the beard. The first few minutes of the film are sepia and I remember my panic and disappointment: oh no, he will be brown, I won't be able to see his blue eyes. And then the woman I wanted to be more than anyone else in the world was on screen: Katharine Ross was another girl crush. After that film, I lusted after straight, shiny hair that swung across my shoulders. I stole even more of Granny Jones's Victorian undies, too, and I would dress up as Katharine Ross alone in my room and practise hair swinging. I remember going to see *The Towering Inferno* later, and agonising for months about who I should pick: Paul Newman or Steve McQueen, Paul Newman or Steve McQueen. As if my decision would ever really matter.

Chapter four

I'm singing, 'Look at that 'at!' in old lady make-up

For some reason that will forever remain unknown, I decided to leave BCHS and the Claw, and the new Sports Hall, and the Dave Hill lookalikes, and do my A levels at Southend College of Technology, located opposite the market and the football club, at the end of a wind tunnel. The catalyst was that Karen Rouse, my feather-cutted best friend, had decided to do her A levels – science- and maths-based – there. Sue had left BCHS, too, after her O levels – she excelled in Latin and Domestic Science – and had started to train as a student nurse in Basildon, a dreadful New Town the other side of the roundabout. I was so relieved when she left home, her things piled in my dad's car. She was still seeing Steve and she wanted her own room, where she could meet him and, I assume, have sex, though she never confided in me about that. I once stopped off at Billericay on the way home from school, and went round to her room, frightening in its neatness, a copy of *19* on the bed. Steve was there, still handsome and skinny. He had left his wife and baby, but now that Sue had him she seemed indifferent to him. It didn't last long after that.

I didn't want to stay at school without Karen, with the swots, the Christines and the Heathers, and so I made my mum and dad take me for an interview with the head of the drama department at Southend, a dreadful, tall, thin woman with over-dyed black hair and an Isadora Duncan dress sense. My excuse to them for leaving high school was that I wanted to study Drama, which BCHS, being academic, did not do. Of course I didn't want to learn acting, especially when I was shown around Southend Tech's facilities. I was dismayed at the mirrors in the dressing room, illuminated with light bulbs, and at the large stage in the hall. I'm not, in any sense of the word, an extrovert. Having gazed at pictures in magazines for so long, what I wanted was to be a model on the cover of *19* magazine, but I couldn't voice this ambition out loud, even to myself, as it was clearly so ludicrous. I was a strange mixture of feeling both hideous and special: not an easy combination. So I told the head of drama I wanted to be a make-up artist and learn to make wigs (I figured that might at least help me look better). 'Those skills will be very useful, as all anyone else wants to do is get a starring role,' she said, sleeves sweeping across my head. 'But you will have to join in.'

I got in. As well as Drama, I was going to be studying A levels in English (taken by Barry Hendry, a Barry Evans lookalike in a biker jacket) and British Politics. I loved studying English – *Antony and Cleopatra*, *A Portrait of the Artist as a Young Man* – but felt I'd spent my life reading about others through words. I wanted action. I wasn't confident as a writer; there was no real flair, although I left with an A and two Bs. I hadn't found my 'voice'.

But on that first day at college, I found it hard to leave my mum at the stone steps to catch the bus. 'If you don't like it, you can just come home early,' she said. When I got there, we filed into the theatre and sat down beside the proscenium stage. I was next to Karen Williams, a big girl in a smock top with a bubble perm and a personality to match. There was a big boy called Martin, an older girl in spectacles with an overbite and really thin arms called Janet, and Caz, a dancer, with over-decorated nails and false eyelashes.

'Projection. It's used on the staaage!' was the first thing the drama teacher uttered to us all, with a flourish. From that moment, I knew I was in the wrong place, on the wrong course. We were forced to improvise. There was a piano and each one of us had to come up with a different way to exit stage left. There were bows and somersaults and cartwheels. When it came to my turn, I was too ashamed to stand up and reveal my lower half and bottom to the watching throng so, as my exit, I kept my bottom on the stool, and exited with it. I was a hit! I was funny! How inventive!

The extrovert nature of all the other students didn't rub off on me but it carried me along in its wake. Karen Williams was a member of an amateur dramatics group called Breadline, and she introduced me to her fellow members: Bob Daws (matinee idol good-looking), Chris Fulford (older than us, with perilously low-slung Levi's, red Kickers and what he hoped was a Marlon Brando T-shirt), Wilma Sweeney (very pretty and overconfident with small brown eyes – from the moment I met her I hated my over-large cow eyes) who had a much older boyfriend and an ambition to land a TV mini-series of one of Jane Austen's books ('I think I have a bonnet face'), and Tracey Sweetinborough, who had diabetes (she looked like a white version of Meera Syal). They all lived in or around Leigh-on-Sea, the posher part of Southend, with its own theatre, the Grand, and a pub on the harbour we started to frequent: the unfortunately named Smack.

I think this brief time was my happiest. I was almost normal. I had friends. I was still very thin – hovering around seven stone – but with my new gang I wasn't as obsessed about what I looked like, mainly because these good-looking, glamorous, ambitious people wanted to be my friends. We would go to a bistro near 'the front', where they would all eat lasagne and drink wine out of bottles covered in rush matting. The height of Seventies sophistication. I, of course, ate nothing, or at least very little. All the boys fancied Wilma. As well as us, there were the older members of the troupe, *Abigail's Party* types with cravats who would host Chicken Marengo parties in their houses, to which Chris would ferry us in his cream Beetle, complaining, 'I can't take six.'

During this time, I was in three wholly unmemorable productions. At Southend Tech, I was Felicity in *The Real Inspector Hound*. My only line was, 'Anyone for tennis?' It's a very funny play but on the first night, in front of a large audience that included 'the gang' (I never told my family I was in a play: I feared not ridicule, exactly, but stepping outside my family role, which was to be the quiet little one in a corner, hiding behind her fringe), our leading lady started vomiting, so her place was taken by an understudy, a shy, entirely untalented girl who walked around woodenly, reading from the script as she hadn't bothered to learn the lines. I got the giggles, which my more actorly friends called 'corpsing'. I just could not stop. I didn't know it then, but it was the last time I'd laugh like that for decades.

In *The Matchgirls*, also part of my A-level course, I was cast as Mrs P. I was duly made up in old lady make-up with an old lady bun, and had to sing a song entitled 'Look at that 'at!' My rendition was more spoken than sung, rather in the manner of Rex Harrison in *My Fair Lady*. I coped with my nerves because my disguise was so complete, I thought no one would recognise me. Only writing now do I realise I was probably playing the Suffragette leader Mrs Pankhurst. That is how blinkered and stupid I was, not even vaguely wondering who on earth Mrs P was and what her motivation was in interfering in the matchgirls' strike for more pay and a way to avoid phossy jaw. This is because all I was interested in was meeting Charles the Law Lecturer.

Now, when I first enrolled at Southend and had my tour,

I was very disappointed to find all the classrooms were flat, with awful chairs with tables attached. I had imagined banks of wooden benches, on a steep camber. But the one bright spot was Charles, a Paul Nicholas lookalike I spotted on my second day who, like Chris, drove a cream Beetle. I wanted Charles, much as my sister wanted Steve. In a year of pining and waiting, head swivelling as if on a stick if ever I spied a Beetle on the high street, I had never once spoken to him. But, after the curtain fell on the very last night of *The Matchgirls*, we all went to the pub on the 'front' to celebrate. Everyone else looked pretty normal. Only I was still in my old lady make-up and old lady bun. Not keen to be left behind, I had followed in their wake, walking against the full force of the wind tunnel to the pub. And there he was. Charles recognised us and came over. I had to turn away, in case he knew it was me; my bun came away in my hands. He never spoke to me or looked at me again.

The third and final production was with my am-dram friends, when I appeared as a mute dancer in a musical at the Grand in Leigh-on-Sea. We even had a photocall in the car park, making the *Echo*. I had to writhe around on stage wearing netting. One review noted I was like a beached fish.

When we weren't rehearsing or travelling up to London by train to see Judi Dench in the RSC at the Aldwych (I, by now, had a mint green T-shirt and white broderie anglaise maxi skirt and brown sandals I thought were the height of sophistication, until one afternoon we all trooped to the King's Road, where girls with black hair wore tartan and Doctor

Martens boots), we were going to the disco. In Southend, there were two – Zero 6, near the airport, and the Talk of the South, or TOTS, on the seafront (The Goldmine, on Canvey Island, was a little bit too far to persuade my dad to come and pick me up). But, for all the Bacardi nights, the strobe lighting and the James Brown records on the turntable, I never once got off with a boy. Perhaps the denim boiler suit put them off. It didn't occur to me how odd I now appeared, especially silhouetted against the relief of the ample Karen: a tiny waist, all angles, like a set square. After the humiliation of being unable to talk to Charles the Law Lecturer and appearing before him as a mute OAP, I was now after Chris Fulford: he had the face of a young Roy Kinnear, but don't let that put you off. He was dangerous. And he was determined to become a movie star.

By 1976, Southend Tech Students Union (a fetid square room, littered with old coffee cups and with strains of 'Bohemian Rhapsody' playing in the background) was also awash with the Persians: dark-skinned young men who had enrolled to avoid conscription back home in Iran. Karen Williams, despite her size, got off with a very small one, Hamid, who lived in a bedsit over a chip shop. I had my eye on Ali, who had an afro and narrow hips encased in tight white jeans. He was just so beautiful. One night, we all arranged to go to Zero 6. I called my mum from the phone box in the lobby to tell her I would be on the last bus. She was in tears. 'Granddad has just been killed. He was knocked off his bicycle. Come home.'

So I went home. I heard on the grapevine that Karen Rouse got off with Ali that night. I would see them, walking arm in arm, like something out of *Love Story*, for what remained of the two years. Their affair spelt the end of our friendship, too. Karen Rouse became the first of many to drop like a stone out of my life; only recently did I learn she had dumped Ali for being too possessive as soon as she got to university. You see? He should have chosen me. It could have been me, except for Grandpa Hewson. There was no sympathy for my mum, only a sense of being thwarted from my grand new life yet again. Why did he have to take that bike ride, why? I learned I was never, ever going to get what I really wanted.

Chapter five

'YOU HAVE REALLY BAD SKIN'

August 1977. Southend Public Library. I'd come in here, in my purple cotton Laura Ashley smock over black flared loons (I'd decided to ring the changes), to escape the wind. There was a copy of *Vogue*, tethered by a piece of string to the wall. On the cover was a model called Kirsti. The price was 60p (it had just gone up by 10p, which was extortionate; hence the piece of string). The cover lines read: 'Ten years after women's lib, Where are YOU now?' and 'Revolutionary new diet theory'. There was no irony in the juxtaposition. Kirsti is wearing a tweed cap, tweed coat, sweater and bow tie, all by Margaret Howell. I wanted, very badly, to be clad head to toe in Margaret Howell. I'm looking at this cover now. I know its contours better than I know my own face. *Vogue* wasn't just a magazine to me, its cover was a mirror: how I wanted to look, dress and *be*.

Inside the magazine, many of the pages are printed in black and white, as it was too expensive to print everything in colour. I ran my finger down the names on the masthead, wondering who these lucky beings might be who had landed such fantastic jobs. I loved the fact they had a 'Contributing Editor, California'. This job title seemed the most glamorous I could possibly imagine. The editor of *Vogue* at that time was the redoubtable Beatrix Miller.

I nearly typed 'Potter', by accident. But whimsical and fond of small wildlife creatures Ms Miller most certainly was not. She replaced Audrey Withers as editor in 1964. Audrey Withers, too, was fearsome: she once wrote in a letter to Cecil Beaton, 'I have unpleasant news for you. We have been forced to kill every picture which you took recently for our April lead. We all found these pictures unpublishable, since they did not in any way embody or put over the theme of our What to Wear with What feature. It has seemed as if you were simply prepared to fit some fashion photography into the interstices of your busy life.'

He replied with, 'I did indeed make luncheon appointments, but then, perhaps unreasonably, most of us indulge in a midday meal.'

Beatrix Miller presided, from 1964 to 1986, over the most beautiful and ground-breaking fashion magazine in the world, helped in no small part by her fashion director, whom she appointed in 1968, the flame-haired Grace Coddington, now at American *Vogue*, the star of *The September Issue*, the documentary made in 2007 on the cusp of the banking crisis.

'"I had an idea this morning in my bath," Bea was always saying,' Grace Coddington tells me. 'One of her best bathroom epiphanies was to disprove all the clichés about how a woman should behave, like, "A lady doesn't put on her make-up in public." And, "You shouldn't dress to be conspicuous in a crowd."'

I knew that the magazine in my lap was where I wanted to be. This is what I wanted to do.

That summer of 1977 was a high point in my life, a K2 of denim-jumpsuit-clad sessions spent doing the dance of the moment, 'the bump', with my best friend Karen Williams, she of the bubble perm and the smocks, to the soundtrack of Stevie Wonder's *Songs in the Key of Life*. I still had a crush on Chris. He made me weak and knocked me off my feet. I felt I was on the *cusp*, and that anything could happen. I was 18 years old, I was in love, I knew what I wanted to do with my life, and I was about to leave home and move to London, just 27 miles along the A127 from Southend, but it felt like the sun: beckoning, bright, exciting and terribly far away. All I had to do was get there. My optimism was nothing to do with the Queen or the Silver Jubilee street parties (I never went to a single one, it was just not deemed cool). It was about being young. About being almost happy.

I had just sat my A-level exams – English, British Politics and Drama and Theatre Arts: who cares, really, about Clytemnestra – but had not yet had the results. I'd taken my studying seriously, spending too much time revising and not enough eating. Inspired by *Vogue*, desperate to be doing something to precipitate my name being added to the mast-head, I had taken to limiting my food for the day to:

One Cal Soup
Nimble bread ('She flies like a bird in the sky-ay-ay-ay')
Poached half a tom (I'd inherited my mum's aversion to
 anything whole or unabbreviated)

I would eschew the nightly tray my mum staggered with into the lounge, on which was placed The Cheese Dish, cream crackers and water biscuits, so hard they could break a tooth. On Saturday nights, to accompany *Ironside*, she would add a festive glass of celery sticks and a little silver salt cellar. I grew to dread the arrival of 'the tray'. I would no longer eat anything that could possibly make me fat. With my Boots calorie counter I knew the calorie count of half a ban, a Ski yogurt (sour!), a slice of Nimble bread that was so thin you could probably read a pony book through it, and an apple. Eighteen years old and I had never had a period. I was still very, very much a virgin.

It was during this summer, driven to Chelmsford to go to Sainsbury's on the precinct by my dad, who now had a second-hand two-seater, pillar-box red MG roadster, having traded in a boring brown Renault, probably aware that soon all his children would have left home and he would no longer have to give them lifts, that I experienced my first panic attack, an affliction that would blight my life for the next 30 years. (I had one last night: I was awake until 3am, watching reruns of *Ab Fab*, afraid I was about to have a heart attack, unable to arrange my thoughts into a comforting night-time story.) We were walking across the car park and I seemed to leave my body and float several feet in the air. I think the panic stemmed not just from not eating, or from the after-effects of spending too much time revising (I can still quote huge chunks of *Antony and Cleopatra*), but realising I was about to fly the nest and no longer be a child. My dad was ter-rified as he watched me go pale and faint, unable to form words and speak: just garbage came out of my mouth, words as simple as Dorothy Perkins and Etam eluded me. When we got home he crossly told my mum that, 'Lizzie is now so thin she has no bottom!' Shy and old-fashioned, that was the first and last time they ever discussed my wellbeing. My mum just didn't want to interfere. As Aunt Sadie said, in *Love in a Cold Climate*, accused of spoiling her youngest: 'Oh, dear, I'm afraid so. It comes of having so many children. One can force oneself to be strict for a few years, but after that it becomes too much of an effort.' Then she asks, 'But, Davey, do you honestly imagine it makes the smallest difference when they are grown up?'

His answer is prophetic. 'Probably not to your children, demons one and all.'

My mum didn't want to upset Daddy. Besides, she had never seen me naked, not recently. I wore baggy layers, huge jumpers. Like most anorexics, I was devious and secretive. I would feed food under the table to Pompey. I would use my vegetarianism as an excuse not to join the others for meals. I complained about the smell of the cooking: I was always opening windows and waving bits of cloth in her direction. How rude, how disrespectful, how puzzling for Mum, a woman who only ever wanted to cook stuff to make me happy.

But I was determined to enjoy my summer holiday because I had my gang, recently joined by the blonde, beautiful Peta Eno, whose cousin, Brian, was in Roxy Music. We were always trying to get her to invite us to her home, in case he turned up. She never would. (Peta got in touch with me not long ago, having seen my name in the papers. She moved to Canada and now has the far more pedestrian married name of Peta McDougall. I have a deep distrust of women who change their names to that of their husband, especially if your maiden name is so exotic and coolly famous. Peta said she was surprised I remember her as beautiful. 'I sadly have not aged well,' she wrote.)

The primary reason for my buoyancy that Jubilee summer, and by that I don't mean the day I bobbed, balloon fashion, like the yellow-trouser-suited model in the Nimble ad, above my black-clad, emaciated self in a car park, was that I had had a letter from *Vogue*. I'd written to the magazine, begging for a job. I wrote the letter on pale blue Basildon Bond paper by hand, as no one I knew owned a typewriter. I had made the life of Miss Miller's secretary, Ingrid Bleichroeder, a misery, with letter after increasingly desperate letter, until she made me 'an appointment'. (Typing Ingrid's name still makes my stomach lurch with nerves and anticipation.) I had received a short, crisp reply, asking me to contact her once I got to London, when she would arrange an interview with Barbara Tims, the managing editor. I was so proud of this letter. My dad was proud of it, too, wielding it in the Wheatsheaf before the Sunday roast, saying his daughter was going to work for a fashion magazine. She was going to make something of her life. I would prove him right.

On 5 September 1977, the last weekend I would spend in my childhood home, my parents rather uncharacteristically threw me a party. I wore a pink cheesecloth shirt dress but then, at the last minute, decided I hated my legs, so added a pair of white Levi's underneath (waist 26in, bought from a denim dive on Southend precinct; they still reeked of joss sticks). Tony turned up by surprise, home from his polytechnic in Bristol, but not Lyn, or Nick or Philip or Clare. I can't remember if Sue came, but if she did, she was probably resentful of my new friends. She was never given a party. I'd asked my dad to illuminate the house outside, so everyone could see how lovely and big it was as they turned up through the big ornate iron gates, and on to the round gravel drive, like something out of *The Great Gatsby*. He spent ages putting up floodlights but, instead of putting them in the bushes, pointing up at the house, he placed them in open windows, so they shone outwards, like something out of Colditz, blinding all who approached.

The gang turned up, including Peta's new friend, a handsome boy called Alan Paveley: he was a sales assistant in

Harrods with the look of the Thirties about him. He was the first to arrive, in fact, and my mum, still baking, had sent him away. He returned an hour later and I was mortified my mum had dismissed someone so effortlessly stylish, the first really fashionable person I'd ever met. He was wearing a navy vintage Burberry trench coat decades before either Burberry or vintage became fashionable, heavy black eyeliner and an earring. I'd never seen a boy in make-up and jewellery before. He took 'Walking in Rhythm' by The Blackbyrds off the turntable and put on 'God Save the Queen' by a band I'd never heard of – the Sex Pistols. My dad promptly made him take it off again. Tony, too, was outraged by punk, equating them with racist skinheads. My mum had laid out a buffet in the dining room: lots of toms and Q and potato salad. Of course I didn't get off with a boy, even at my own party. I remember standing alone, near the French windows, no one to talk to.

Two days later, ferried by my dad, who'd had to hire a van, I was in London sharing a flat in the Barbican, a concrete edifice built on the ruins of the Blitz, near St Paul's, with Bob, Chris and Karen, all about to enrol as drama students. Chris was talking about going that night to see Blondie, someone I'd never heard of. My mum had waved me off without a tear. I told her I would be back every weekend. Maybe she was relieved – now it would just be her and Daddy? I never really gave a thought to the fact she'd be alone each evening, while he still went to the pub.

I was too caught up in moving to London, escaping the number 11 bus and the Southend Wind Tunnel. The boys had their own rooms, Chris's decorated with Salvador Dalí posters and a mysterious wooden 'unit' we were all barred from opening, while Karen and I had to share. There was a wraparound balcony, a waste disposal in the galley kitchen, and two shower rooms. After the spiders and the cold in Rettendon, it was heaven: £16 a week each. I unpacked my few things, while Dad hovered, anxious to leave. I was wearing a small, green T-shirt covered in rabbits. It was a child's T-shirt. Mum hadn't asked if I was going to eat while I was in London. For the first time, I would have total control over my calorie intake. I was elated.

We thought our flat's address was prophetic: Number 4 Shakespeare Tower. Paul Raymond lived in the penthouse. The others were desperate to be famous, while I just wanted to work at *Vogue* and write captions beneath photographs of Janice Dickinson. Meanwhile, I had to catch the tube from Moorgate to the Elephant & Castle every day, where I was taking Media Studies at the London College of Printing, my lecturer a failed *Daily Express* subeditor in a powder blue safari suit. I'd applied, desperate to work at *Vogue* and not knowing anyone in the world of magazines to give me advice, by sending in my last school project, a history of fashion, mainly inspired by the costumes on *Upstairs, Downstairs* (I would gaze adoringly at the visage of Lesley-Anne Down). My interviewer asked how I would turn that into a feature for a magazine. 'I have no idea,' I said.

'We train journalists, not fashion stylists,' he said.

'Perhaps I should have brought you *Trendy*.'

I knew then I could never be a proper journalist, talking to people who didn't want to talk to me. I was already partially deaf, which meant I became anxious if anyone spoke to me. I knew I was boring and had nothing to say. I was even in awe of the other students, all of whom were overconfident, fearless. There was Carole, on the radio course (now a BBC political correspondent), and I know she looked down on me. We once had to learn how to interview someone on camera and, when they played my segment back, I was so shocked at how I looked and sounded I knew I would never be able to be out there, in the open, exposed, let alone on TV.

It was early one autumn morning, in those first few months in London, that I had my second panic attack. Waiting on the tube platform, I realised I could no longer read the signs on the opposite wall, the inevitable *Time Out* posters telling me all the things I could do, if only I were braver, lovelier, richer, better connected. I thought I was going blind. I later realised the blindness was due to lack of food – I was by now perilously thin, trying to make myself acceptable, ready to take my place at *Vogue*, once I had escaped the Elephant & Castle.

Unfortunately, even though we now shared a flat, Chris completely forgot about me once he found his new drama school friends. One afternoon, I returned home to find him in bed with Josette Simon, a fellow student, on the brink of fame in *Blake's 7*. Her high, round bottom haunts me still, and must have set my nakedness back by several decades. He eventually moved out to live with Joanne Whalley. There is nothing more crushing than being passed over for a diminutive, smoky-voiced new star with dark, liquid eyes, who would become a national heartthrob in *The Singing Detective* and *Scandal*. I was crushed. Flattened. I was never more thrilled than when Val Kilmer hove on to the scene. But I pretended to my sister Sue that Chris was my boyfriend. She came to see me one summer weekend. She had made up a hamper so we could go and sit in Regent's Park, before watching *A Midsummer Night's Dream*. It was really heavy, given she had packed it with so much food. I wonder she'd thought Chris would carry it but, of course, he was at work, backstage at *Bubbling Brown Sugar*, trying to earn an Equity card. So we lugged that hamper and Sue became more and more bad tempered. I'd promised we would have free tickets to see *Brown Sugar* that night, as Chris had said he would arrange two comps. We turned up but he had forgotten to leave them on the door. She travelled back to Billericay, convinced I was living in a fantasy. It's true, I was.

But there were good days in the autumn of a silvery year that was fast becoming tarnished. My extrovert actor friends hosted lots of parties. Lyn came along to one, finding her way improbably from yet another 'nursing home' (she was now at the National Heart Hospital in Westmoreland Street), and got off with Bob and became so drunk she later told me she found herself back in her bedsit, fully dressed on the floor, 'but still holding my handbag'. Chris invited his Central School classmates, including Rupert Everett. There were all these handsome budding stars standing in the galley kitchen, but not one of them fancied me.

We did have something in common, though; if not ambition, then at least making the most of what we had. Exercise, which I had performed furtively to keep off the pounds, was suddenly fashionable among my set, positively *de rigueur*. A very handsome young man called Nick, also from Southend (they came like moths via the portal that is Fenchurch Street Station), told me he had just started doing something called Pilates at The Place on Euston Road. 'Really, it's better than the gym because it gives you a dancer's body: long and lean, not muscly and bunchy.'

'Yes!' added another friend brought along by Bob, whom he'd met at RADA. Her name was Pamela Dillman, daughter of Bradford, star of *The Swarm*; Bob eventually married her. 'I go to jazz classes and tap in Covent Garden. You really have to come along.'

Pamela Dillman was so beautiful: dark, with huge eyes, like a young Natalie Wood. I wanted to be like her. I wanted a long and lean body more than anything else in the world.

And so it began. My obsession with exercise, with being long and lean and lovely. I would run, round and round the ornamental gardens below our flat in the Barbican, near the fish pond. I would jog on a Saturday all the way from the Barbican to Covent Garden or to The Place on Euston Road. I bulk-bought Lycra. I went to ballet shops and bought pink tights and pink leather ballet pumps. When I bump into people now who knew me then, they always tell me the one thing they remember was that I was always jogging. 'You ran around Leith Links at all hours of the day,' one woman told me. I'd been in Edinburgh, visiting Tony, who had moved there to be with his soon-to-be-wife, Laura. At a wedding of a colleague in 1981, I'd pounded the lanes around her house in Scotland, afraid the whisky-sodden air would make me drunk. I was never drunk. Not then. I was too controlled. Whenever I went anywhere, I would take my jar of decaf coffee with me, just in case anyone offered me caffeine. I never drank tea. I saw hot drinks as a sign of weakness. No wonder I never had a boyfriend.

I liked the studio at The Place the best. It was ripe with the smell of sweat and there were rats and cockroaches in the changing room: I felt this was authentic. Two former ballet dancers ran the Pilates studio. I would warm up first on a tiny, bouncy trampoline. My limbs, every inch of them, were covered in legwarmers. I wore ballet tights the colour of my mum's dentures, and nylon baggy bloomers over the top, which were meant to help make you sweat.

And then came the machines. It looked like a torture chamber. The plié machine was my favourite. Up and down. Up and down. Each time, the stomach was pulled in, to the floor. This would produce 'core strength'. There were straps and pulleys and weights and giant triangular cushions you would squeeze between your knees. I did this for an hour and a half, three times a week, not to mention body conditioning classes, jazz tap classes and ballet. At The Place, I would lie with my bottom against the glass of the mirror, legs wide apart against the glass. The teacher would place sandbags of weights along my inner thighs. This would 'open' them. The pain was indescribable. Of course, I understand why dancers do this: they need flexibility and range. But why was I doing this? I never danced, not since 'the bump'. It was all about punishment, about being better.

As Beauty in *Vogue* put it so eloquently, 'Exercise is a very important part of reducing.'

Each day all I ate was a free sample of peanut butter off a teeny coloured plastic spoon at Neal's Yard Wholefoods in Covent Garden. Sometimes, late at night in my narrow divan in my shared bedroom, I'd be so hungry I had to creep to the kitchen, stand on a chair, and steal some of Chris's Original Crunchy, which he hid in a top cupboard (he noticed, though, and it disappeared to be locked in his 'unit'). If we ever went out to a pub, I drank only Tab, never alcohol, because I had read in *Vogue* that alcohol was 'empty calories'. I became known for always eating half a banana, leaving the other half in its folded-over skin in a cup. Occasionally, feeling festive, I would grill half a tom.

I lived on £20 a week, as my dad never contributed to my grant: did he just not have it? I never felt confident enough to ask. I never demanded, which made me just like my mum. He did lend me his Access card, though, for essentials: I bought two stainless steel coffee cups from a catering shop (I still have them), two white catering plates, some bed linen and a towel, as I didn't want to take Pompey's. A couple of years later, my dad wrote me a letter, asking for his money back. I reread the letter, barely able to believe what it said in his neat blue script. I had always been good! I never asked him for much! Why have children if you don't want to help them? I wonder if my mum read it, or asked him not to send it. I felt shocked, and then frightened. I was determined never to ask a man for money again.

I earned extra money by babysitting in other flats in Shakespeare Tower and its neighbour, Cromwell Tower. Chris would always turn up, chirpy, rubbing his hands together, half an hour in, and raid the enormous fridges: as the owners were invariably American bankers, with hard Wassily chairs, their fridges were always stuffed with meat loaf. I still wonder how these parents ever squared the shy, skinny girl who looked after their child with her evidently enormous appetite. I found it hard to say no to Chris, always wanting to please him. Every night, in the corridor of our flat, with its brown-and-white Seventies shagpile carpet, Chris would perform his sit-ups, hundreds of them, and my job was to hold on to his cherry red Kickers. I felt I was a non-woman, which was true, given the lack of periods, but I so wanted him to take my face in his hands and tell me he had always loved me. But, like every other man I ever came across, he just used me. 'Can your brother Philip get me digs in Cambridge when I go there to do rep?'

There were two other boys in our group. The first was Russell T Grant (he added the 'T' to avoid being muddled up with the astrologer), the most breathtakingly handsome boy I had ever met. He was Jewish and a cockney. Chris introduced me to him in the pub next to the Palace Theatre on Cambridge Circus. I kissed him at a party once, and the next time Karen was away, he stayed the night in my single bed. I was too terrified to have sex, so he just slept. I lay awake all night, rigid, afraid to move. So this is what it is like, being horizontal with a boy. How amazingly intimate, his skin on mine. Do people do this night after night and get over how abnormal it is? What if my mum knew?

In the morning, I got up, showered and dressed, and made breakfast. And I waited. And I waited. I went back into the bedroom and he had fallen asleep. It didn't occur to me to wake him up, to impose my will upon his; I was a weed in the wind, waiting to be wafted or trodden on. This is how the Cresswell family must have felt when they sat waiting for me to appear for our trip to the zoo. So much effort and angst on my part, so little on his. I pretended he was my boyfriend for a while. We went to a wedding together once, me in a green bouclé wool vintage jacket from Kensington Market. This is what real life must be like for normal people, I thought, content just to stand in his aura. But it wasn't to be. He became tired of the fact I was too scared to have sex, mainly because I knew my body was too hairy to be seen. I went home for the weekend and he appeared on the *Generation Game*, and became mildly famous for saying, 'Glass bottle, bottle glass.' 'Is that your boyfriend?' my mum asked. 'Yes,' I replied. 'Yes, it is.'

The final male member of our group was Tim Walker. He was at RADA with Bob: he had the wiry head of Sid James and a huge Roman nose. He was the first openly gay boy I ever knew. He would sleep on Bob's floor and dream of stardom. I once went to see him in *Timon of Athens* 'in the round' at Stratford, and fell asleep rather obviously in the front row. We'd have great fun with Timmy: we'd act out the parts in *Fawlty Towers* (I was always Manuel), and do synchronised dances to the soundtrack of *Saturday Night Fever*. When I had my first journalism job interview, I wore a completely brown outfit from Topshop, along with a heavy, hand-knitted waistcoat with leather buttons bought from Miss Selfridge, and a brown leather cummerbund. Timmy pronounced I looked like 'an expensive piece of shit'. He was only joking but his words stuck in my brain. I will never, I thought, escape from Essex, escape from being either a plate or a boy.

There was just one more friend on the scene – a young woman called Sue Needleman, who was on the same acting course as Karen, at Middlesex Poly. She lived in Mill Hill with her parents and I was hugely impressed that in her garage was a Rolls Royce. She had Victoria Principal hair, a Louis Vuitton handbag, and was never out of high heels. She also had a car, which we all found useful. She would come and collect us, and we would go to see *Star Wars* and *Close Encounters of the Third Kind* at the Odeon Leicester Square. Sue was a veteran skier and persuaded me to go with her in the winter of 1978. I had no money, so borrowed some from my reluctant dad, who would later write another letter, asking why on earth I had felt the need to go on holiday. (Well, to make up for the one trip to Jersey, is what I wanted to say. But I didn't.) We were going to Montgenèvre, on the border between France and Italy, sharing a chalet with two young families. Can you imagine an 18-year-old settling for such an arrangement today?

I had no kit, so borrowed a pair of salopettes from Alan Paveley's gay friend, Graeme. He lent me a pair of ski gloves, too, but they had a hole in each thumb. A super-confident blonde chalet girl, who had probably been born on skis, picked us up from the airport. We arrived at the chalet and discovered we would be staying in the basement, sharing a room. It seemed to be my fate, to always share a room with another girl, like a superannuated *Malory Towers*. The chalet girls obviously thought dusting our room, which we soon christened 'the hell hole', was beneath them. The children of the two families christened me Lorraine Chase, who was big at the time for her advert featuring Luton Airport, but I was much, much thinner. I was now only six and a half stone.

Sue Needleman, with her big hair and pink snowsuit, glided everywhere, expending no effort at all. I was hopeless, plus I found skiing unbearably cold, given the holes in my gloves and lack of body fat. I fell off the button lift into a snow drift and had to be rescued. The rescue team told me they had only been able to find me as they had heard me swearing.

The high point was the village disco, which we frequented every night. There we met two French boys, Michel and Albert, on a working holiday from Paris. I was attracted to

Albert, as he seemed to have a dangerous quality. He was stocky, quite short, hair the colour of digestive biscuits. His first words to me were, 'What does "Steer it up" mean?' They were playing a Bob Marley record. I mimed stirring a Christmas pudding. On the slutty chalet girls' night off, we'd all been told to eat out, so we knew the dreadful families would not be home. We four trooped in the snow back to the chalet in our moon boots. I finally felt my life was about to start.

We sat in the living room and Sue brought drinks. Albert then led me down to the hell hole. He got undressed and I noticed his feet were filthy. There was a really strange smell, but I was too afraid to say anything. Both he and Michel worked in a hotel, in the kitchen. I was about to have sex. 'Oh, thank you, God. Thank you so bloody much!' I got undressed, having first turned the light off. At this stage, I was 20, but my breasts had not yet grown too big and pendulous, and I had yet to cut them off, creating hideous scars. I had not yet had veneers glued on to my teeth, nor ever dyed my hair. I was 20 years old and the cold mountain air had dried up my terrible spots, caused by a lack of nutrients from the dieting and the over-exercising. Looking back, this was a pivotal moment. My life would have taken a completely different course if the night had gone well. I would have realised I was normal, and not quite so hideous, if a handsome Frenchman had found me desirable. There was very little kissing and not too much fondling, which might have had something to do with what happened next. But I was too naïve to demand anything, initiate anything. He placed the head of his penis against my vagina. He pushed, I braced, he pushed again, but he couldn't get it in. He tried again. Nothing. I was impenetrable. He swore in French. Eventually, he gave up. I was mortified. All that yearning, all those posters, so much bulk-buying of Blu-tack, and I was not able to have sex.

What was wrong with me? Perhaps there was a mistake in my anatomy? Perhaps that is why I had never menstruated like all the other girls at BCHS, even the ugly ones and the useless ones who were never chosen first in netball and rounders, the ones who wore glasses and had horrible wiry hair. I don't have a hole. I wonder if anyone thought to check when I was born? Ten fingers, ten toes, the right number of orifices? I doubt it because LOOK AT WHAT HAPPENED when I finally let go, when I finally decide to DO IT, let my hair down, forget my morals, became sordid! This never happened to Edna O'Brien. Or Clare. Or Lyn. Or even Sue! I was not like other girls. I was impenetrable. ('How do women get raped, against their will?' I thought on the plane home. I wouldn't even be able to be attacked! I wasn't good enough biologically to be a victim!)

Albert put on his socks, covering those dirty toenails, and then his pants and trousers. The smell abated now it was covered in fabric. I pulled on my clothes, embarrassed not to be a woman at all. I was a Sindy doll. I was useless, not just at forward rolls and climbing the rope, but at performing the most basic function of a human being. Millions of people have done this! Even my mum managed to do this: she must have done! We went back upstairs, not exchanging a word. Sue assumed we had had sex, and I didn't disabuse her. It would be nearly 20 years before I saw a man naked, and prone, again.

If only someone had talked to me about sex. This is what happens. This is what a man has to do. It isn't a reflex, like gagging or a cat landing on its paws, you have to learn what to do. You must demand this, this and this, like a super-naughty shopping list: half a mo, and stroke me here. You need to get to know your most intimate regions, using a mirror (oh, that there had been *Sex and the City* and Samantha in those dark, unenlightened days). You need to get drunk first (I wouldn't even partake of the fondue since it was a melted cheese and wine concoction in which you dipped pieces of bread – it sat on every table like a vat of fat). Part of it must have been his fault. But there was no one to talk to about this problem, yet another one to add to the already long list.

Was this brief encounter the reason I overcompensated so wildly when it came to men in future years? Here, have a car. Have a music review column in my magazine. Have a mixing deck and speakers. Have half my house. Come on holiday to Jamaica/Thailand/Puglia/Babington House/Firenze/Paris/ New York/Dublin. Because I Am Not Like Other Girls. I am no good at sex. I am not normal. I have to TRY harder. I once had a friend, Jenny, not a particularly beautiful girl, or clever, she didn't have a great job and lived in a tiny house with bad furniture way outside London, past Croydon, but she once dated a man so he would MOVE A LUMP OF CONCRETE from the front of her house! And he did it, too. But I have overcompensated for the whole of my life, giving men things – cashmere V-necks from Harrods and Burberry buttery leather blazers and Jil Sander sweaters bought from Colette in Paris and Rolex watches with pink faces made in the year they were born and bicycles – all because a kitchen hand with dirty feet had never been told by his French mother, a woman supposed to know these things, about FOREPLAY!

Sue Needleman and I saw the two handsome *garçons* on our last day, bombing down the slopes on their day off. '*Salut! Voulez-vous un rendezvous?*' shouted Michel. But we never saw them again.

It was at one of the now-legendary Barbican parties that Alan Paveley, who had given up being a punk and become one of the first New Romantics (he was always knocking things over with his sleeves), pushed me into Chris's bedroom and kissed me against the mysterious 'unit'. As he broke away, he told me that back home in Southend I'd been known as 'The girl least likely to . . .'

'Least likely to what?' I said.

'Do anything. Succeed. Give it up. Have sex.'

I was devastated. That statement, knowing what others really thought of me, has stuck in my mind. It was true, though. I'd tried very hard to have sex and failed. Oh, the shame. How did Karen, with her bubble perm and smocks, do it, and Auntie Olive, and not me?

It was Alan who introduced me and Karen to the Blitz club, a dreadful dive in Holborn. We would go along to Bowie night, frequented by Boy George, his friend Marilyn and various members of Spandau Ballet. Alan, aware of my extreme poverty, offered me his job as a coat check at the club. I would sit in this cupboard, night after night, on a stool (I have never got the hang of stools), wondering why I was never being handed any coats. It was the Wheatsheaf children's saloon bar all over again. Surely, I thought, someone should be wearing a jacket or an anorak, as it's nearly winter. But these people were far too cool to ever wear coats.

I was in my second year at LCP when I finally plucked up the courage to dial Ingrid and tell her I was at last in London. She granted me an appointment with the managing editor of *Vogue*, as she said she would. I wore a loose-knit, baggy white sweater I'd bought in Topshop and a pair of royal blue needlecord (!) trousers I'd got second hand. I couldn't afford a coat or a handbag; anyway, girls didn't really think about handbags in those days. The moment I got inside the lobby of the building on Hanover Square I realised I was woefully inappropriately dressed: there was a lot of what I recognised as Halston, Gucci, Fiorucci. I had stepped into a pop record. I sat in Miss Tims's small but immaculate office and, from the pained expression, I realised my accent, honed on Canvey Island and Leigh-on-Sea, was wrong, too. I became desperate, knowing before she even spoke that my dream job was out of my reach.

'I am afraid the only avenue open to you is to enter the *Vogue* talent competition,' she said, snapping her diary shut.

'But I'm at journalism school! Why didn't somebody tell me about that?' I asked, but I had already been dismissed. It was the WHSmith Win A Pony short story contest all over again – my vain attempt as a child to fill the rough side of the lawn with a real, live pony. I never got the pony, despite the fact I entered every year. I never got a gold star, or a Highly Commended. I never got the job on *Vogue*. I might as well have been dressed as a tampon. I was the sartorial equivalent of a saucer of soil.

But I could still live out its pages, and do whatever it told me to do, no matter how hard or extreme or unnatural. Which is exactly what I set out to do.

In October 1978, a *Vogue* issue was published that changed my life. (It has 'October 1ˢᵗ' printed on the spine, as in those days *Vogue* often published twice a month, with other editions, too, including Beauty, Health and Slimming in *Vogue*, and *Vogue Patterns*.) Janice Dickinson is on the cover with her brown, Galaxy Counter eyes, bee-stung lips and slightly blobby nose. It is not an exaggeration to say I fell in love with her. I wanted to be her. I could not stop gazing at her. She was me but infinitely *better*.

As I starved and exercised, I started to dress exclusively in baggy clothes and pile on make-up to cover my deteriorating, grey and lifeless skin. I had developed a beard and a moustache, as long, black, wiry hair took hold, my body trying to stay warm against the Arctic assault of starvation; either that, or I was turning into a man.

But this look – all black hair and Siouxsie Sioux black eye make-up above a cadaverous body clad in a PVC donkey jacket I'd wrestled from a dustman – somehow suited the times. I decided, given the blasted Ingrid and the ineptitude of the safari-suited journalism lecturer (my first story was an exposé of the cruelty of polo, when I had managed to hold Prince Charles's pony, but this heady high soon deteriorated into pieces on the London Transport Lost Property Office and learning teeline, shorthand I would never use), that the only fast track into fashion was to become a model. I knew I wasn't beautiful; I'd had plenty of evidence of that. Boys never fancied me, or chatted me up, or wolf whistled. But I had to be in the pages of *Vogue* somehow. I still didn't look at myself in the mirror, but I had fabricated in my head a version of myself that was very like Ali MacGraw. I was commendably thin, though no one ever commented. Apart from just one boy, called Nick, a medical student who came to one of our parties. Slow dancing with me, he felt how bony I was, how my hand-made leather trousers hung from the bones of my hips, like curtains, and he wondered whether I should really be that thin. I shrank away from him and realised why I never let my mum or dad hug me. They would have found out: anyone who touched me would soon find out.

I kept my ambition a secret, of course. I took a bus to Notting Hill, to the Electric cinema (then unrefurbished and riddled with mice) to watch a documentary on modelling. Oh, how I wanted to be in that world. I decided I simply had to go and see, on what I would later learn was a 'go see',

Laraine Ashton, then the biggest model agent in the business, a fact I had gleaned from *Vogue*.

Above the hopeless journalism course at the London College of Printing was the photography department. The boys there were much better looking than the budding hacks (the only student on my course to ask me out was a 50-year-old Nigerian). I had my eye on Mark, who was blond, drove a Mini, and wore an angora sweater. One day, by the lift, I told him I was going to see a model agent, and asked if he could take some test shots for me. Should we meet for a drink to discuss? I would pay him, a transaction that from this moment would define every relationship I ever had. He agreed to the 'date' – we stood on sawdust in a pub, overlooking the water of St Katherine Docks, me not knowing what to say or how to act – which ended improbably back at the Barbican flat. As I said goodbye to him at the door, he leaned to kiss me. I gathered he wanted to have sex with me, but was repelled rather by Karen's still, sleeping form inches from my bed. But he stuck to his word and agreed to take my test shots. I borrowed a yellow, checker-paned sweater from Alan, and Karen's boyfriend's leather jacket. One Sunday afternoon, we met up in St James's Park. Mark had me holding on to trees and looking moody, like a bipolar chimp. A while later, he sent me the contacts, all in black and white. I couldn't look at them, but on the back of one he had written, 'Sorry they are all a bit blurred. This one is my favourite. Marcus x'

Hope soared. I ignored the pretentious new name. Too scared to forewarn Ms Ashton by booking an appointment,

I took my portfolio along unannounced to the agency's HQ in the West End. I remember pressing the bell at the door, thinking the world was about to open, too, like a flower.

Laraine Ashton, a former model herself, with a curtain of ironed hair, sat me down, barely looking at the photos. 'I don't think you're quite right for modelling,' she said, trying to let me down gently. I was still smarting from what Alan Paveley had told me and so I persisted. Normally, I would have just agreed. 'I know,' I would have said. 'I might have Ingrid Boulting's eyebrows, but my face is a spoon.' But, desperate, knowing my life was going nowhere, I persisted. I'd not starved myself for nothing.

'But why? I'm young, I'm slim, I'm tall. I was Miss Zero Six! [I was, I was. The gang had made me enter, and I'd won, shaking, blind with fear. But the competition wasn't really up to much: a lardy girl in a Laura Ashley smock and a shy girl with a feather cut and a lower set of teeth that lapped over her top ones. My prize was an invitation to take part in the regional final, but I was too scared to turn up.] Please, I'll do anything. I just want to be in *Vogue*.'

'I'm sorry,' she said, standing up. 'But you've got really bad skin. You should see your GP. You need steroid cream. Your face is weeping.'

Later, so was I.

The ups and downs of that Silver Jubilee year, which turned me from a contender into an also-ran, left me as limp and unwanted as tattered bunting, ripped in the breeze. But Alan was right – I was the girl least likely to. Even 'Marcus', my gigolo, turned down my advances, telling me he only ever dated black girls. I was always the wrong race. Later, I tried to persuade a neighbour, David Scrace, to go out with me. I even learned squash so I could invite him to play a match. Which he did. After the game, he handed me his racket and asked if I could take it home for him, as he had a dinner date with a Filipino. It hadn't occurred to him I was anything other than a blob, a eunuch. My whole life has been spent trying to prove them wrong.

I longed to join the Sanctuary in Covent Garden, viz.: 'Give the body a break and take a glass of redcurrant juice, 65p. Lie on the black cushions and suck thoughtfully through coloured straws and crushed ice, flick idly through magazines and newspapers provided. Indulge further in delicious massage with extract oils, £10, manicures, facials, waxing, eyelash tinting, etc. The effect is shattering.' Yes, it truly can be.

But I was too shy to enter such a place, be looked at. Yet I still didn't give up. I posted one of Marcus's photos to a modelling competition run by *Honey* magazine. I put my name, age and address on the back. I'd been spurred on after I attended my first ever fashion show: the Mulberry collection, at the Hard Rock Café near Hyde Park Corner. A boy on the LCP radio course invited me along. He was not attractive, but he had a car and was already working part-time for local station LBC, as he had a posh voice. So I went with him to see Mulberry and, while I loved the clothes, all striped tanks tops and silvery grey blousons, I loved the models with their straight, shiny hair and straight, shiny chests even more. This is it, I thought, I am finally where it's at! I longed to be plucked from my life and just stand there, like them, not having to talk to anyone. So I posted off the picture of me grasping on to a tree branch, for all the world like a leather-jacketed simian, but I never heard back. One day, my photo was returned. I remember tipping the brown envelope upside down and shaking it, in case they had written me a note, saying I was now discovered. It was empty. My relationship with modelling was like the one I had with ponies. I wanted to be Chloe in *Riders from Afar* and so, even though I didn't have the nerve or the skill, sometimes throwing up before a riding lesson, hardly able to wait until it was over, legs like jelly, when I could at last dismount, I drove myself to ride because I wanted to be other than me. Life would have been so much easier if I'd been content to be mediocre. I forced myself only to fail.

Even though I was only a student, I would walk to South Molton Street, lured by the sirens at *Vogue*, to shop and to get my hair cut and given a 'vegetable rinse', hoping for a glimpse of Kerry at Molton Brown, a name I'd learned from studying the microscopic photo credits in *Vogue*. I'd buy Molton Browners – bits of wire covered in foam and fabric – and twist my hair in them, having a very prickly night's sleep, but managing to attain the dark, curly locks of Andie MacDowell as she looked on the cover of *Harpers & Queen*. (I wrote to *Harpers & Queen* for a job, too, and received a cross note back from the editor, Willie Landels, telling me off for addressing him as a Miss.) My first designer purchase was a blue snowflake cotton sweater from Joseph Tricot (this was before the Moroccan-born retailer opened his chain of high end boutiques). It started a pattern, not just a snowflake one, but one of buy now, wear now, still hate yourself for not being happy, pay later.

Another Mecca in late Seventies London was not the arse end of the King's Road, where punk was still lurking, but the far smarter Beauchamp Place, just round the corner from Harrods (Way In!) in Knightsbridge. Here were my twin altars at which to worship: Crocodile, a boutique selling not only Maud Frizon but Calvin Klein. I bought a pair of olive silk shorts and a cream silk knit sweater. I spent the next decade paying off the debt on my store card.

The second altar was the Hawkins Clinic on Beauchamp Place. This was run by a fearsome, ancient woman called Countess Hanna Jankovitch: she was always lurking in a white coat at the top of the narrow, steep stairs. I was there to help cure my terrible acne, brought on by my anorexia, which had the side effect of suppressing any feminine hormones in my system, allowing testosterone to wreak havoc, and to treat the tiny thread veins on my face that were stopping me from getting dates: all paid for on credit. I figured I was saving money by not buying food.

The thread veins were almost imperceptible to the human eye, but as Janice didn't appear to have any capillaries in that cover photo, I felt mine had to be eliminated, too. The countess sold me a tiny pot full of an unguent made from the crushed shells of snails, with a tiny blue drawing of a snail on the lid, at over £200 a pot. This was supposed to cure me, but of course it never did. She would cauterise the tiny veins in my face with a fine needle. This treatment left my face riddled with browns scabs, like a liver-coloured Dalmatian.

I spent a lot of time in Knightsbridge in the last two years of the Seventies. I once had dinner with Karen in Mr Chow, hoping for a glimpse of Tina Chow, then a model, or my ultimate female fantasy, Marie Helvin, but all I got was a phenomenally large bill. I also went every week to the Tao Clinic at 153 Brompton Road. The ad in *Vogue* read, 'Superfluous hair. Ever wished it could be removed once and for all?' Well, yes! In this clinic were row upon row of green curtained cubicles, exactly like *M.A.S.H.*, but then this was the war on superfluous hair, that most shameful and secretive of female afflictions. Electrolysis then was painful and expensive. I had it on my face, between my breasts and around my nipples. Again, my extreme emaciation had allowed the male hormones to run riot, turning me into a bear. Even now, as I drive past Harrods, a frisson of dread creeps over me, and I put my foot down on the accelerator.

Chapter six

PLUCK, JOG, EX, TAN

Four Cox's apples or sim (get Berwick St Market)
One Loseley Yogurt, rasp. Hazelnut if faint, blind or
    blackouts
7st 4lb
Pluck, jog, ex, tan

It's like a very unfunny page from a Bridget Jones novel.
Let me translate. I ate apples throughout the day to stave
off hunger pangs (they stripped the enamel from my teeth,
which meant I would later have to invest in expensive
veneers). I would buy a yogurt from Cranks. If I was feeling
faint, when the world would go dark and I was barely able
to see let alone stand, I would choose a hazelnut flavour,
as this had 35 more calories. 'Pluck, jog, ex [for exercise], tan'

is at the bottom of every page during this period (don't be silly, I was still not privy to periods).

Each day I would pluck hairs from my chin, upper lip, breasts, bikini area, knees and stomach: the Tao Clinic clearly deserved to be sued. I would jog, of course, that is self-explanatory, but I would also have to 'ex': I devised an exercise routine for use at home, with leg weights strapped to my ankles, as well as attending as many Pilates and body conditioning classes as I could afford. It is interesting, too, that I wrote the word 'tan'. Perhaps I was one of the first fake tanners; a hyper-grooming pioneer. I did so because I wanted the olive skin of Janice Dickinson. An early product was Guerlain's Teint Dore, which would wash off and smelled of rose petals: my sheets were permanently stained, like an ungodly Turin Shroud. I would do anything to change my identity. I even hated my name and my voice: a nasal, uninteresting drone, which means I often won't speak so that others will be spared it. (Today, now that I interview celebrities, Detective Columbo-style, I employ someone else to transcribe the tapes so I don't have to hear my awful, Kenneth Williams honking.)

Ten years of eating less than 300 or 400 (depending on the size of the Cox's apples) calories a day finally took its toll. When I walked outside, I couldn't feel the pavement. I was always cold, dressed in layers so no one would notice. But all the other dancers in my exercise classes were like this: wrapped in layers. The skin on my face, despite the countess, was still oozing. I remember lying prone on my plié machine at The Place and the instructor, Gordon, having moved over to supervise the exact turnout of my feet, looked at my face and said, hand clasped over his mouth, 'Oh, my God!'

Asleep one night in my narrow, single, resolutely virginal bed, I could not control my thoughts. It was as though my brain was a scatter-gun. I could not form a sentence or remember anyone's name. I couldn't picture Pompey's face. I was terrified. I couldn't move, or open my eyes for fear of what I might see.

But the moment that made me at last go to my GP to try to tackle my anorexia arrived in a class at the Pineapple Dance Centre, my spiritual home, the altar upon which I sacrificed myself. Someone called my name (I was known as 'Libby' by the dance teacher, so tired was I of being Lizzie or Liz); I looked up and caught sight of my legs, encased in pink ballet tights, in the full-length mirror. I gasped when I saw my body. Hip bones like those on a long-dead corpse dug up from a bog, jutting obscenely. Great big knees below thighs that were like a cartoon of a skeleton. I ran out the door and into the arms of the National Health Service, never to emerge again as me. The whole me.

I booked myself an appointment with a consultant at a specialist clinic. I wish I could remember his name, it was Professor something, but perhaps I have blacked it out. He was inept, disinterested, or maybe back then there was no understanding of anorexia. Nobody offered me any help in the form of counselling, or even a sympathetic chat. No one asked, 'Why?'

First, I had to lie on a hospital trolley. I was asked to expose my genitals. I had never been naked in front of a man before in broad daylight. I was terrified.

'Have you ever had a period?'

'No. Not really.'

'Have you ever had sex?'

'No! I did try, once, but it wouldn't go in.'

He then inserted his hand into my vagina, and broke my hymen.

'There. At least that's over with.'

I wasn't aghast, I was relieved. I have a hole! I was then weighed: 6st 1lb (I have never liked odd pounds, it always had to be a round number). People tut tutted. The professor sat me down. I was told to eat three meals a day and have sweets in between. I was to be weighed every week and, if I did not improve, then I would be admitted, force-fed high calorie slush, my parents would be informed and I would jolly well do as I was told. I was also prescribed steroids, which I took, as I didn't think they contained any calories. This turned out to be the biggest mistake I would ever make.

And so began a cycle (I did actually cycle, too, to burn more calories, until I was knocked off my bike by a maniac turning left without signalling outside the Houses of Parliament) of me being weighed in out-patients once a week. Two days before the weigh-in, I would eat peanut butter and banana sandwiches from Neal's Yard, homity pies ('vomity', Sue called them – garlic, cream and potato in a pastry case; a cacophony of calories, a party of protein) and nut rissoles from Cranks on Broadwick Street (the rissoles were fried, which to me was as bad as eating an avocado, i.e., riddled with fat) and cheese baps filled with mustard and cress and lashes of butter. All of this was not to stave off death, which I never thought about, but to stave off the interference of the NHS. I never enjoyed this food, merely steeled myself to swallow it. I would sew bottles of water into the red lining of my navy Paul Smith men's coat, which I would refuse to take off. Fear had driven me to the hospital, but my bigger fear was being fat. If I can feel my ribs, I'm pleased, still, today. I want thighs like Gandhi. If there is a gap at the top of my legs, I feel joy, no matter what else is happening around me. Even at my thinnest, I still had a tiny pot belly, so I would lie on the floor, performing sit-ups. As a child I'd watched a yoga programme on TV hosted by Richard Hittleman. *Yoga for Health* featured two beautiful women in coloured leotards with matching tights, long, straight hair, and long, straight limbs. One was called Lynn. I loved Lynn. I would contort myself as a child, in private, in front of the telly.

The nurses were pleased I was putting on weight. What they didn't know, apart from the fact I had inserted water bottles about my person, was that after I was weighed, I would starve myself and exercise even more diligently – four-hour body conditioning class, cycle, run, ballet, then Pilates. The Loseley yogurt lid would remain unfurled, unlicked. I enjoyed fooling the doctors. I felt pure, infinitely superior. If I felt I was going blind and mad again, I would eat half a banana. Never a whole one.

But then one day, stepping triumphant off the scales in my Paul Smith coat, I must have made a loud whooshing noise, like the sea, as the water lapped within. A matron patted me up and down, and revealed my subterfuge. The consultant was summoned. Oh, dear. I must be punished. I was admitted there and then, placed on a ward with lunatics (there was no eating disorder unit) and incarcerated for six months. Not even once during this time was I asked why I wanted to starve myself to death. It was terribly lucky I had by now finished my journalism course and was unemployed.

But oddly, I felt safe. My little side cabinet was neat and flawless. I had a view of the square outside, could hear the men in the meat market nearby calling and shouting early each day. I could smell the blood on their white coats. They were like giant, slow-moving sanitary pads. I no longer had to go outside, something I found scary. I had become increasingly agoraphobic. I no longer had to get dressed, or put on make-up. I no longer smelled like rose petals, as my limbs no longer had to be nut brown. I didn't have to talk to anyone. I let the whiskers on my chin grow long: they gave me something to play with, knit. Still do. (Oh, the joy of being single, sitting on a sofa, endlessly feeling, then tugging and pulling one from its thick, woody root, holding it up to the light, seeing it shine and bristle. Repeating the pattern.) My feet became soft from not walking. I didn't want to leave my cell. I had complete control of it. I looked down at the nurses, who always seemed to be chomping on something, making cups of tea, stirring. How workshy.

My mum outside her mother's house, aged 20, in a balloon-sleeved coat. Love the jaunty hat.

My dad in a cricket sweater while at Hampstead School, before he acquired the lifelong 'tache.

My dad in Rome during the Second World War and, right, with some of his tank regiment buddies.

My mum, alone for most of the war, with her first born, Clare. New mothers these days just don't look nearly as well groomed.

Left: In the Potteries after the end of the war. Mum and Dad with Clare, new baby Philip, and the bulldog. Note my dad's cravat, and the exaggerated shoulders of my mum's coat.

Right: In Africa, Dad with Clare, Philip and Lyn in a nurse's uniform. Josephine is at the back.

Outside the Officers' Mess, left to right: Clare, Philip, Nick, Lyn and Baby Tony. Right: Clare with Bruce, the Dalmatian.

One of the many postcards my dad sent, first during the war and later from East Africa. He still signed his name 'Bert' to his mother, but to everyone else he was already 'Robert'.

Me being held by Granny Jones in her garden in Mill Hill and, right, with a giant teddy I was not allowed to keep, which must have belonged to my cousins.

My christening in Mill Hill, with me on my mum's lap, next to Granny Jones, with Sue in the centre, Tony crouching gingerly in front.

'The two little girls'. A Rettendon Primary School photo, the only one my mum ever purchased, with Sue and me in our homemade pinafores.

Rettendon Place: I think it beautiful now, but at the time it was cold and gloomy. I would never mount the stairs at night on my own.

Mum and Dad sunbathing in Jersey, my dad exposing his Cary Grant tan, and, right, in the garden at Rettendon, clearly still very much in love.

Again at Mill Hill. My dad is in the doorway, head always tilted on one side after he fell from a ladder. I'm next to my mum in a dress she made me, trying to pull it down over my thighs, while Sue is standing in a tank top, feather cut and pink suede shoes. I was about 12 years old.

At Philip's wedding. I'm holding a plastic clutch bag to hide my stomach.

On holiday in Jersey with my rather exhibitionist school friend Frances. I did not take off my jeans and towelling top for the duration. Note my hand flying up to cover my face in the picture below left.

Brentwood County High School photo, taken in the art room. I am back row, far right, next to my best friend, Karen Rouse. Gillian Saunders is beaming blondely, middle row, far right.

Nick, drinking special beer he brought with him (he was very particular) to my parents' semi in Saffron Walden, for a party to see Lyn off on her way to get married in Sydney.

Me, Sue and Tony's wife, Laura, who would later die of alcoholism, leaving behind her two young daughters. I'm in the Paul Smith men's coat I would use to secrete bottles of water when being weighed at the clinic.

Mum and Dad at Tony's wedding in Edinburgh. I made this dress worn by my mum, from silk bought at Liberty; I have since lost this skill.

Me, Mum, Sue and Labby at our cottage in Saffron Walden. I'm in my mid-twenties and still had my breasts at this point, wearing a Katharine Hamnett baggy shirt to conceal them, and leggings.

The abortive modelling career. This is the photo taken by 'Marcus' in St James's Park. You can't see the acne, so perhaps Marcus was an early exponent of air brushing.

Mum and Dad on holiday in Devon, and Mum, below, in the lounge, knitting.

Discussing the ethics of stealing a man's sperm on *This Morning*, after my article in the *Daily Mail*.

In the garden in Hackney with Nirpal, shortly after we were married. I'm wearing my cream wedding tuxedo trousers, in an embrace that was both awkward and rare.

The body image debacle. At the government summit with Tessa Jowell, sitting on my left, and the offending cover, right, featuring an airbrushed Sophie Dahl.

But if you think anorexia is not suicide, think again. It is. The slowest, cruellest kind. It is a fix, and we starvation addicts are tougher than anyone hooked on heroin. We don't think we are right, we know we are. We view people who eat, the chubby, as weak, as messy. I never enjoyed Christmas as a child because I was always worried my mum would assault me with a tartan shortbread tin, its lid open, a mirror to my big fat face. Being thin made me other, apart, special, superior, clean.

Even as a patient, I fooled them all. I wouldn't swallow what I ate and, as I was a vegetarian, they were limited in what they could feed me. I told them it was against my religion to eat what they offered, which made them back off a bit. Even then, I was able to have a friend smuggle in *Vogue*. 'Fasting is not dangerous, but an 800-calorie-a-day diet for a longer period is a more certain way of slimming.' Yes, you see, I am right because *Vogue* says it is right. I disappeared into the magazine's glossy pages during my solitude: my favourite model now was Sloane Condren, photographed by Bruce Weber in 1981 on the prairies of the Wild West in white petticoats, no make-up, hair in a nest. I loved Talisa Soto, too. The Louise Brooks bob, the dark eyes, the linear body, the lovely life, surrounded by adoring men.

I was discharged. I weighed 8st, the heaviest I had ever been or ever would be. But I wasn't cured. I went home, back to the Barbican flat, and planned my new regime. Pluck, jog, ex, tan. Pluck, jog, ex, tan. Less is more.

But of course my undoing was the steroids. They made me

take them, but they didn't tell me what they would do to me. If I didn't take them, I would have to be admitted again. The steroid was progesterone, one little white tablet a day. Well, I thought, this is better than being given food. It's so tiny! But my breasts, which until this moment had been dormant, began to grow, due to the disgusting, bovine hormones in the drugs. By the time I realised this, it was too late. I had udders. Big, ponderous teats.

Feeling brave, one evening I stood in my original Seventies bathroom and took off my pale pink Topshop T-shirt and bra. My breasts were pointing down towards my belly. They were covered in purple veins. How could this have happened to me! How could I ever do modern tap again? Or be naked in front of a man? I decided I had no choice but to have them cut off one day . . .

Having left the London College of Printing with no journalism job in sight, not even one solid lead, no relative with connections I could call on and no skills to speak of, when I got out of hospital I applied for a job as a secretary at a firm of architects in the Barbican. The man I worked for was ghastly, a dwarf, who never ceased to be amazed at my ineptitude: I'd hear him yelling at other people, telling them how useless I was. There were no such things as a photocopier in those days. Instead, I had to use this big cylindrical machine in the basement to make copies. I was no good at typing, despite the valiant efforts of the safari-suited lecturers at the LCP to teach us to touch type. I hated the job so thoroughly,

I would write endless applications to the vacancies that appeared each week in the *UK Press Gazette*. One was to be a reporter on John Craven's *Newsround*. I composed my application and attached the required photo. I was shocked to be invited for an interview and got a series of buses to the BBC Centre in Shepherd's Bush, sweating all the way with fear. I hadn't slept the night before. My thespian flatmates teased me that I would be on the telly long before they were. I was interviewed by two bright male Oxbridge types, who told me I hadn't got the job, but they'd been intrigued by my photo, in which I had held my head at a weird angle. 'We just wondered if you were always in that position.' And that was it. All that effort for nothing. I returned to blacken my fingers the next day on the wretched copying machine.

I finally left the dwarf when I managed to get a job as secretary to the headmistress of the Arts Educational School, which was located in a beautiful old building just a few steps from the Barbican underground car park. I ate only porridge each day, as I could afford nothing else (and anything else would instantly make me fat). The head was kind, distracted, but I hated the children: extrovert, ringleted, Bonnie Langford types.

But one journalistic application was, finally, successful. It was to be a reporter on *Lyons Mail*, the in-house newspaper of the Lyons company and its ice cream and tea factories in West London. My boss was Peter Pound, a very old-fashioned gentleman with brilliantined jet black hair, three-piece suits and an office on Ridgmount Street, just off Tottenham Court

Road. I shared his room; in fact, sitting all day with my back to him, I was the sole employee. My main task each week was to take the page proofs on the number 9 bus to the Lyons HQ in Hammersmith, and then catch the bus back again. I didn't write anything, although I did go to the ice cream factories, donning a hair net, to interview some of the employees. My copy never went in. Peter Pound also published a magazine called *Entertaining at Home*, but I wasn't allowed to go near this very sedate quarterly. The job was so boring that I would spend most of my day, when Peter Pound was out, phoning the *Top of the Pops* hit line to listen to a crackly Adam and the Ants single down the telephone, over and over again. I read books, too, dozens of them. And could barely contain my excitement as *Vogue* publication day came round, and I was able to go to the newsagent and buy my copy, and study every photograph.

The irony of my working in this little room, occasionally venturing out to don a hairnet in an Acton factory, and my dreams of working at Vogue House, was not lost on me.

Chapter seven

'PINEWOOD STUDIOS HAVE BURNT DOWN? OH NO! ALL THOSE TREES!'

Eventually, after applying to an ad in the *Guardian*, I got an interview at *Company* magazine. This was based at Broadwick House in Soho, in the same building as *Cosmopolitan, Harpers & Queen, She* and *Good Housekeeping*. I walked into the lobby and there were giant billboards of all the latest covers on the walls. I felt I had arrived. I had long read my sisters' *Cosmopolitan*s, but I never really fell in love with the women on the cover: Farrah Fawcett and Christie Brinkley. They were too confident, too glossy, too artificial, too blonde. I simply did not want to be them. But I thought I had more chance of a job on *Company*. Launched in 1978, its team were all ex-*Cosmo* staffers who wanted to capitalise on that brand's fame and success, and publish a version for younger readers. The editor was Maggie Goodman, who had a bubble perm and a slightly nervous, shy manner. She interviewed me, along with the production editor, Maggie Koumi, a more brittle woman. I know for a fact that Maggie Koumi rejected me for the job as junior subeditor, on £3,000 a year, because, frankly, one hair-netted photo of me in *Lyons Mail* was not much of a track record. It was Maggie Goodman who took pity on my keenness.

Being a subeditor was about the lowliest job it was possible to get bar working in the post room, or on reception. You didn't actually write anything, apart from captions, and even these got changed by those higher up the food chain. There were no computers and, I'm afraid to say, I wasn't important enough to be allowed to use a typewriter. An article would be faxed in by one of our writers, or dropped off by hand. My job was to cast it off, which meant work out how many words long it was. This you did by ruling up each page – literally drawing a pencilled line, trimming off the uneven words, counting the words in a line and multiplying it by the number of lines on a page. Then on each page you counted the words cut off by the ruled line. You did this for every page. Once you knew the length, you could then let the editor know and she would map out the flatplan, allocating pages to stories. You would make pencil marks on the copy, correcting spelling and punctuation, and then, at the end of the day, you would send it in the big bundle marked 'Typesetter'. If you changed your mind about a correction, you would underline the deletion with a dotted line, then write the word 'stet' in the margin, enclosed in a circle. This was like typesetting time travelling, correcting past bad decisions. I wish I could stet my life now.

The copy would go off to the typesetter and then be returned a few days later as 'galleys': long strips of type, either jagged and ranged left, or in a block, which was called 'justified'. My next job involved being given a paper layout by the art department. This was headed by the wonderfully exotic Nadia, who was Greek and who was then nurturing a gangly South American photographer called Mario Testino, who would sit on our desks and make us laugh. I would have to cut round each galley and paste the words on to the page. If it was too long, which it invariably was, given the method of counting, I would fold up the over-matter. This was then cut, by scrawling through words or sentences, on another copy of the galley, and sent away again. By this time you were sick of the article you were working on. You then had to think of a heading and an intro or 'standfirst'. Anything I wrote was inevitably changed at the next, page proof, stage.

There was no creativity, on my part, involved in the process at all. I never expected to have any input and felt, instead, probably because of the deep-seated fear of being run over, that I was lucky to be allowed to touch any of this stuff. To sit in a room papered with photographs of Andie MacDowell and Brooke Shields – that was *enough*.

Eventually, after a year, by 1982, I was given the responsibility of '*Company* Counsel'. This was the section at the back, mainly just columns and columns of type, giving our readers advice: on careers, relationships and their civil rights (our agony aunt for this last topic was Patricia Hewitt, who would later become a government minister). I would dispatch readers' letters to the experts, await the bundle of replies, have them made into galleys, then put them on the page, very often according to length. There were many times when I published the same letter and answer twice. Or three letters on almost identical topics. It was all about making it fit.

What I enjoyed most was the camaraderie among the all-female (bar Panos Pitsillides in the art department) staff. I knew every intricate detail of these women's lives. There was Pam, who was married with a baby, Fiona, who was Scottish and had a family castle, and Bridget Freer, secretary to the editor but who wanted to break into writing. Linda Kelsey was the deputy editor but, despite sitting just a few feet away from me for many years, I found her too terrifyingly beautiful to speak to or even look upon. She had a breathtakingly handsome husband and they would have dinner at L'Escargot.

Did I want to write? I once compiled a 'Pop Quiz'. This horrendous one-page article remained in my portfolio when applying for jobs for the next 20 years, though I can't think why. It had questions such as, 'Who are the two members of Soft Cell?' But you have to remember the standard was not very high then (although the December 2012 *Vogue* had another pop quiz in its pages, which is surely scraping the bottom of the ideas barrel). We once ran a feature where we asked lots of famous pop stars, including Duran Duran and Nick Heyward (from Haircut One Hundred), to whistle. Bear in mind this was before the internet and interactive features with ... sound. I was sent on two press trips, which for someone who had never been further than Jersey and Sidmouth were like manna from heaven. The first was to Torquay, the 'Riviera of the south west', to publicise a new spa. I had to take a tennis racket, trainers and a hard hat for pony trekking on Dartmoor. While I was there, I had my first pedicure, my first beauty treatment. I could not get over how wonderful it felt to have someone massage my feet. Wow! This must be what it is like to have a real boyfriend. The second press trip was to a Greek resort called Vasiliki, on a windsurfing holiday. Not the most apt assignment, given my stone-mimicking swimming ability, but no matter. I shared an awful room with a blonde girl with huge breasts and a deep tan, and tasted Greek yogurt for the first time. That was a revelation. The windsurfing, however, was a disaster: I would wail in the warm shallows for my instructor to come out and hold the board still while I clambered on. Weak from barely eating, I couldn't lift the sail from the water. My knees have still not recovered. But the piece was published in the travel section, a narrow strip with no photos, just my small by-line. I was shyly proud of this small piece. I wanted it to be funny, but it just came across as self-deprecating.

Then I got my big break: an interview with Kenneth Branagh, who had just left drama school. He was appearing in a TV series about the Troubles in Ireland, and I had to catch a train to his awful rented house full of house plants (I hate indoor foliage) to talk to him about it. I'd been taught shorthand by the dreaded LCP, but it evaporated once I was finally faced with an actual subject. I couldn't read back a word of what I had scribbled during my tongue-tied interrogation, so I had to get in touch with him and ask the questions all over again. But the piece was published in 'Dispatches', at the front of the magazine, under the heading: 'The Boy from Belfast'. It was all of 300 words. I duly cut it out and had it mounted on a show card, such as you see by the side of shoes in shops, trumpeting publicity.

I also interviewed a schoolgirl from Hampstead called Rachel Weisz. She had just modelled for the annual teenage edition of *Harpers*, which was only next door to us, over a partition, but it might as well have been on Mars, for all the contact there was between editorial teams. *Harpers* was almost as good as *Vogue*, but much posher. The young women who worked for it were terrifying: I'd bump into Amanda Grieve, later Lady Harlech, the Chanel muse, shopping in Cranks and the sight of her, all black bob, wide mouth and crazy black clothes, like a crow, put me off my pot of macro rice (300 calories) for good. There was Angel Bacon, too, a blonde Amazonian who worked in their art department. I started to feel that *Company* was the home of rejects.

I organised something called a 'Company Wheel In'. This was designed to raise money for charity and was to be a bike-a-thon and roller-skate-a-thon in Battersea Park. I was in charge of conscripting celebrities; which I duly did – all three members of Bananarama and both members of Dollar. My mum and dad drove all the way from Essex to support me. The sight of my mum chatting politely to Thereza Bazar still makes me incredulous. 'What do you do, dear?' she asked, handbag held, Queen fashion, over the crook of her arm.

We rarely put a celebrity on the cover but if we did, she was usually dead, such as Marilyn Monroe. We didn't put gifts on the cover, either, unlike *Flexipop!*, a magazine I was rather fond of which gave away flexi discs. That was how I got my first copy of an early record, 'Young Parisians', by Adam and the Ants. I was still in love with Adam, after those crackly, one-sided phone calls in the office of *Lyons Mail*, and set out to meet him. I persuaded my editor to allow me to interview his backing dance group: black, male dancers who went under the name Masaai, probably incorrectly spelt. I don't think one of them came from Africa. They were leaving London to go on tour with Adam and his Ants, and I was going with them! We all boarded the train from King's Cross together but, for the entire journey, I didn't see Adam Ant or his wretched dancers once. We got to the venue and, again, I didn't get to speak to Adam. After the show, we all went to the hotel and, I think, for a few seconds I glimpsed Adam far away along a hallway, disappearing into his room.

The publicist said Adam had wondered, 'Who on earth you were.' And that was it. No interview. No article. I had to try harder.

So, I put in for an interview with the man himself and it was granted, given I had promised the record label PR, a breed of human who would blight my existence for the next 20-odd years, five pages in *Company*. I finally met Adam, real name Stuart Goddard, one morning in a deserted pub on Westbourne Grove, which was a dangerous, unglamorous place back then. He was not wearing any make-up and looked so different, sort of ordinary, that it put me off. My questions were hopeless: 'Do you know Malcolm McLaren?' was one early shocker. And, 'What do you think of Siouxsie Sioux?' I told him I loved *Jubilee*, the punk film directed by Derek Jarman, in which he had played the silent, brooding Kid. He was having none of being flattered and seemed an oddly morose young man. I asked him about his wardrobe of clothes and his relationship with Vivienne Westwood. 'One day, it will all be in the V and A,' was all he would say.

I left the interview feeling ugly and deflated, a mixture of emotions which has remained pretty much the default setting after every such celebrity pairing since. I realised that a man you might think you are in love with can fail even to see you, let alone bring it upon himself to ask you out. But still I didn't give up. During our weekly ideas meeting (a memorable one was when the new chief sub, a sexually charged, energetic woman called Susan, who had no real affinity with the pernickety job of deciding whether a sentence needed a semicolon or a colon, suggested a column on the inside back page called 'Back Passage'), I piped up that, when I had met Adam Ant, he had offered to give me a guided tour of the clothes in his wardrobe. 'Really?' said Maggie Goodman. 'That is fantastic!' Five pages were duly earmarked 'Adam Ant's wardrobe' (surely the most interesting feature that month, given the Simon Le Bon whistling debacle, although often the lengthy novel extracts were wonderful). I had no hope in hell of persuading Adam to do this, given his frosty farewell and silence since, but I basked for a week or so in the fact that my feature was getting five pages. Eventually, the words were rubbed out and I returned to '*Company* Counsel' and Patricia Hewitt and the big jars of cow gum we used to stick down the galleys.

I don't think my reputation ever recovered from this. But I didn't learn my lesson, and probably still haven't.

We published a fashion spread featuring a gorgeous, long-haired Italian male model: one photo had him posing in a biker jacket. I was hooked. I found out his name by rummaging through the desk of Elaine, the fashion editor, as models, even those featured on covers, were never credited back then. It was Christopher Siragusa. I had to meet him. I called his agent and said I wanted to interview him for *Company* magazine. The meeting was duly set up in Kettner's, the pizza restaurant on Romilly Street; surely the last place you would ever choose to meet a model. We had lunch. He tossed his long hair rather a lot. A few days later, he was on a 'go see' at *Harpers* next door, so he came in to see me. I was at my desk cutting out galleys and he floated towards me, long, parachute silk, Katharine Hamnett shirt following in his wake, feline, languorous. Every jaw in the office dropped to the hideous carpet. I stood up. He kissed my cheek. I didn't know it then, but this moment was the zenith of my life, romantic and corporate. 'Hey,' he said. I steered him over to the chairs near the blue partitions at the front of the office and we sat, me trying to make painful small talk. 'Did you hear Pinewood Studios have just burnt down?' I asked him. 'Nooo,' he said, almost tearful. 'All those trees.'

Somehow, I managed to persuade him to come to my house for dinner. I'd left the Barbican flat to rent one room in a house in Barnes for £10 a week. It was so cheap because I had to babysit four nights a week for the young couple who owned it, and it was just a room in the attic with a shower cubicle. There were no cooking facilities. But I loved living in Barnes next to the river. I would jog along the towpath every morning with the family's golden retriever, Buster, and then catch the number 9 from Barnes Bridge to Soho, which took the scenic route across Hammersmith Bridge and past the clock at Harvey Nichols. I'd get off at Piccadilly Circus, then sprint up Regent Street, turn right into Carnaby Street, then full of leather skirts and political badges, and into the office. But living in one room of a house with a couple and young family proved difficult, given the only opportunity I had to play 'Young Parisians' was on their record player, in their smart front room, when they were out. I'd sit in my garret every night, the only highlight watching *Brideshead Revisited* on the tiny portable TV. I once had some friends to lunch on a Saturday while the family were away on holiday. They arrived home right in the middle of it and treated me as if I was breaking and entering. Another time, I set fire to a tea towel, probably while feeding their small child, and soaked it in bleach in a saucepan overnight to resurrect it. I was given my marching orders. I was 'far too untidy'.

So now, just in time for my date with the supermodel, I was living in a two-up two-down in Brixton, opposite a slum clearance area, and next door to a prostitute. I'd bought it with my sister Sue, by now a nurse in Hammersmith suffering from depression, mainly I think from living in a nursing home near the flyover. I had felt sorry for her and, having been evicted from Barnes, I needed someone to share the mortgage with. We had done it up with Laura Ashley sprigs on the walls and curtains; an oddly rustic motif given the location.

Christopher turned up at the door, an improbable peacock in a hen run. I made him stir-fried vegetables, but he told me off for using low-fat margarine to fry them in. I must buy extra virgin olive oil, something I'd never heard of. Sue hovered for a while before leaving for night duty. 'Is that a nurse's uniform?' Christopher drawled. He left straight after the meal. But I still didn't take the hint. I called him at home – this call took great courage. There was no answer. But I knew where he lived – in a mansion flat in Knightsbridge, almost opposite the Brompton Oratory. I turned up and rang his doorbell. Nothing. I rang again. A Pre-Raphaelite head leaned out. 'Oh, hi,' he said, curls slowly bobbing, disappearing back inside again. *And he never buzzed me in.* That was it. I had turned into Penny Cresswell, left waiting for someone who was never to show up. She never got to the zoo. I never got my second date. It simply never occurred to me that he was gay until about 30 years later.

Chapter eight

'THE QUEEN MUM IS NOT IN HOSPITAL'

Having toiled at *Company* for several years, I could no longer survive on the salary, despite the fact I still didn't buy food. I applied to the London *Evening Standard* to be, yes, again, a subeditor. The man who interviewed me was called Seamus and he was, predictably, Irish. I entered the marbled hall of the Art Deco building on Fleet Street, having cycled to the interview wearing the black PVC dustman's jacket. I also wore a black leather A-line skirt from Carnaby Street and Maud Frizon suede peep toes with a small heel. My test was to edit a small news item and give it a heading. That was it. A few days later, I got a short note. 'Liz, you're on.' It was not a proper job, though, with holiday pay and a pension, merely a six-month contract. At my leaving party, Maggie Goodman said she could not possibly compete with Fleet Street but that I had emerged as a dark horse, given a Sicilian-American supermodel had turned up at my desk one day and I had persuaded Dollar to attend a charity 'wheel in'. My present was a silver chunky bracelet with a huge black stone from Butler & Wilson on South Molton Street. I felt very anxious, leaving such a cosy place for the all-male environs of Fleet Street.

And it was tough. Not the work, which mainly consisted of subbing a couple of hundred words every few hours or so; Fleet Street was awash with money and vastly overstaffed. I would scribble a heading on the daily 'Shopping Basket' column about where to buy the cheapest potatoes, place it in a plastic tube, which was then inserted in the pipe above my head. Hot air sucked it down to the composing room, where men I never met would turn it into upside-down, back-to-front hot metal. Being assigned to edit the 'Shopping Basket' was, in hindsight, sexist. And, while a rose was left on my desk every morning by some probably red-faced, drink-addled hack, no one ever harassed me. But there was lots of swearing, using the name of my former imaginary pony. And the hours were crippling. I had to be at my desk at 5am and was often left on my own in the office, late at night, while all the men went to the pub, to write the billboards that would be placed by the tube station entrances and exits. I would also have to man the tickertape that spewed out news from around the world. If anything earth shattering occurred, I was to write an NIB (news in brief) and a billboard to advertise this exclusive. Imagine my nerves as I sat there, possessing no judgement whatsoever about what constituted a good story. My usual response, to a story such as 'Princess Diana is pregnant', was to ignore it. But, reprimanded once too often, I decided to be more gung-ho. One night, over the tickertape came news that the Queen Mum was in hospital. I composed a NIB, not even knowing what the correct protocol was for addressing royalty in print, and a billboard – 'Queen Mum in hospital!' I'd added the exclamation point after several years of creative thwarting.

The next morning I was called to the desk of Seamus. (In my time there I never once clapped eyes on the editor, Louis Kirby, or indeed any of the top brass.) 'The Queen Mother is not in hospital.'

'Oh, good. Is she much better?'

'She has never been in hospital. Not recently, anyway.'

I had picked up an old story, God knows how. Why had I not checked it with the Palace? Well, my only relationship with the phone was performing three rings back home to Rettendon, and my abortive phone call to a Sicilian-American supermodel. I was far too scared to call the Palace. In fact, it had never occurred to me to do so. I was sacked. I got on my bike back to Brixton. (I heard, sometime later, that Seamus had gone totally mad and had had to be removed from the office, using restraints.)

But Bridget, a friend from *Company*, had a boyfriend – a big hulk with weird teeth called Martin – who worked as a sub on *Woman's Realm*, a dreary weekly magazine full of recipes, knitting patterns and historical romantic serials, and they had a job going. The publication had been born in the same year as me: 1958. Perhaps this was a sign. The editor was Judith Hall, a tall, patrician woman. The chief sub was a bubbly red head called Sally Sheringham. I was given an interview. 'Why do you want to leave Fleet Street?' she asked me, in the office at King's Reach Tower, a brown Seventies monolith by the Thames at Southwark. I didn't tell her I'd been sacked. She took me on.

I didn't want to tell anyone I was now working on *Woman's Realm*, which once published a photograph of a Christmas pudding on the cover with the cover line: 'Knit your own Christmas pudding'. I felt it was almost as bad as working on *Lyons Mail*. The main problem was that I had to edit the knitting patterns (as well as complete knitted outfits and trousers, we had patterns for knitted Dickensian mice and Hobby Bears), in which I had no interest whatsoever, not even a passing one, and it resulted in elderly women the length and breadth of the land finding themselves in terrible knots. (When the magazine was shut down in 2001, the then editor explained, 'We tried to change the magazine but it is still associated with knitting, even though we haven't carried patterns for six years.')

Woman's Realm was owned by IPC, which also published *Honey* magazine on a floor several storeys above my own. It was heavily unionised, which meant every week we received a reading allowance, in cash, in a brown envelope. You could only get a job as a secretary or in the post room if your father was a member of the print union. There was a vast canteen. But rather than the heady heights of *Cosmo* and its centre-folds, we had our own vicar, Roger, as a columnist. And, oh my God, the recipes. Each Christmas, we would publish a complete countdown to Christmas Day, making everything from scratch, and which would kick off around October. It was a very bad idea putting me, a recovering and frequently lapsing anorexic, anywhere near this gargantuan exercise, a project that had been mapped out since spring by our team of home economists, food stylists, table dressers, candle lighters, crystal polishers, tablecloth lace makers, quilt square ironers and so on. It was the practice at the time to put all measurements in both imperial and metric. I was far too interested in Way Bandy and Kerry from Molton Brown, both stars of *Vogue*'s weeny cover credits, to be bothered with measurements for ingredients. And so I got the metric con-versions completely wrong, adding a nought as I was unsure of where on earth the decimal point should be. Needless to say, I was soon looking for another job.

This came in the fine form of Patrick, chief sub of *The Sunday Times Magazine*. I had already had one piece pub-lished in this august tome, then the pinnacle of British journalism. While still at *Company*, I had interviewed Rupert Everett, who I had met back in the galley kitchen of the Barbican flat and who was then starring in *Another Country* on stage and soon in film, for the 'Life in the Day' slot at the back of the magazine. The woman who had trusted me with this venture was the LITD editor, the redoubtable, meticulous

Susan Raven. It was duly published. Rupert telephoned me to say that because I had written that he sometimes leaves his Bywater Street house to buy a paper wearing just his underwear, and is always drunk, the director of his latest play wanted to sack him. It was an early warning: be careful what you write. Obviously, I took absolutely no notice.

Patrick offered me casual work, four days a week, on the subs desk. Looking back on that first day when I joined the team in the building on Gray's Inn Road, there were seven other subs working on the weekly magazine. The telephones rang constantly, so much so that when I went to bed that night, I could still hear them ringing in my ears. Philip Clarke was the editor and David Robson the deputy. The only women high up were the deputy chief sub, Liz, a tall, red-cheeked woman who had just bought a new Golf and whose mother was dying (there was, given the high staffing levels, much idle chatter), the wonderfully named Sarah Spankie, and Sarah Miller, who once commissioned and edited a page on all the different types of make-up brush you could purchase (she now edits *Condé Nast Traveller*). That page took about eight weeks to perfect. Everyone took long, boozy lunch hours. Editors would often return late in the afternoon to sleep with their heads on their desks, ignoring the furiously ringing telephones millimetres from their ears.

Did I mention the perfection? The art department would give us a layout, on which we had to attach the 'A matter', as the intros were called at *The Sunday Times*. There were still no computers, just small typewriters. No photocopiers, either, but 'blacks', which you would take using carbon paper every time you wrote something. The layout would include a dummy heading and dummy A matter. I would have to write all the 'signposting', using the exact number of characters dictated by the art department, men who seldom read the actual copy. You could not write an A matter with two consecutive lines of the same length: each line had to go in and out, by the prescribed amount.

While features by the likes of Jay McInerney and Edmund White, and photos by the likes of Lord Snowdon and Henri Cartier-Bresson, often took months to produce and tens of thousands in expenses, the penning of the heading and A matters could take equally as long, if not longer. But I did have some triumphs. A cover interview with David Puttnam, who had just failed as a Hollywood studio boss, had my line: 'The lost tycoon'. A fashion spread of brown clothes for autumn had a standfirst, penned by me in a rare flash of inspiration, that finished with the now immortal: 'Brown is the new black.'

It could have been a bit ridiculous, all the humming and hawing, the endless revisions, were the results not so outstanding. But the writers were nothing if not divas. Jay McInerney once called for my head for placing asterisks in every one of his childhood imaginary ponies. As a subeditor, I became nothing if not meticulous, terrified of making a mistake. (In a long interview with Melvyn Bragg, I had allowed 'alter' to slip through instead of 'altar'; I still lie awake at night, regretting this error with every fibre of my being.) Georgina Howell was our star interviewer and I was deeply in awe of her, given her victory in the 1960 *Vogue* talent contest, and subsequent employment as that magazine's features editor. She had written an interview with fashion designer Ossie Clark. It was my job to edit it, fact check it, and get it 'on the page'. Hmmm, I thought. I am going to make Georgina Howell in awe of my meticulous attention to detail. I got hold of Ossie Clark's telephone number and, more importantly, his fax number. I faxed the entire feature over to him. I remember, now, standing at that fax machine, watching it light up like Christmas, swallowing each densely typed page. I sent him a note: 'Do let me know if there is anything you think might be inaccurate.'

The next day, I was called into David Robson's office. He was a kind man, an old-school Fleet Street type who probably knew change was in the air: he could have sniffed it, were the office not so full of Capstan Full Strength smoke. Ossie Clark had slapped an injunction on the magazine, the first in its history. Why on earth had I faxed the article to him? Did I not know that the last thing you ever do is warn a subject about what is to be written? Um, no, I did not. Amazingly, I wasn't sacked. But I learned something: to place a curse on anyone who slighted me. Ossie Clark was later murdered by his gay ex-lover, so you can see it worked.

There were lots of other scrapes, near disasters and lessons. I was, by now, having given up on marrying Adam Ant, in love with Prince, and *The Sunday Times Magazine* was offered an interview and shoot with his protégée, a rapper called Cat, who was going solo, also on the Warner Brothers roster. The fearsome PR Barbara Charone, a thick-set American lesbian with a Bette Davis drawl, set it up. The photographer was to be Snowdon. The writer was to be me! I turned up at the Chelsea Studio wearing a John Richmond skin-tight black top, with white lettering along the arm, a style first popularised during Prince's *Lovesexy* tour. Prince's music was on the speakers but Snowdon thought it was a racket and asked for it to be turned off. Cat Glover was gauche, sweet and clearly completely untalented. Her album, produced by Tim Simenon of Bomb the Bass, was a disaster. But my interview with her was even worse. It included the line: 'This is one hot fairytale.'

The woman editing my piece, a big-boned, Joyce Grenfell doppelgänger called Hannah, went into the office with all the male bigwigs. The result was not good. 'They want you to write about how it was working with Prince, how it felt to be in the studio with him. They want to feel the sweat from his brow.'

I rewrote the entire thing in tears. The finished article was okay, but it wasn't brilliant. As David Robson said to me, 'It's good, but it's not poetry.' I resolved to try harder.

I was relegated to writing tiny boxes for the 'Just Testing' section at the 'back of the book', which is what we called the arse end of the publication, where John Diamond, later married to Nigella Lawson and who would go on to write a column about his fight with cancer, also worked.

Back at home in our house in Brixton, Sue, who was on a diet, would make endless curries and soups. One night, she left the curries to cool in the kitchen and I left the door open.

She was furious – one of the two cats we'd inherited with the house might, or might not, there was always that possibility, have sniffed them. 'I will have to throw them all away!' she shouted, scraping them into the dustbin.

When, one night, we noticed our front window had almost been jerried open, she panicked. She called our brother Nick, who immediately came round, put up window locks, and slept for a few nights in the front room. But she wanted to move out of London, to work at Addenbrooke's Hospital in Cambridge. I agreed to move with her and commute. After all, it meant I could get a horse; I'd always dreamed of getting a horse. We got a joint mortgage, difficult at the time if you were a woman, both on a minimum wage, so the interest was 15 per cent.

While Saffron Walden was lovely, the move was a big mistake. Huge. It took ages to get to work and the fare was crippling: always paid for on my American Express card. Because it was a two-hour commute away and because I dreaded the walk, the tube ride, the train journey and then the cycle home, I would start to linger in the office until late. I noticed all the men would do this, too. Only the women would speed out the door at 6pm, no matter what was going on, no matter who had died or who had triumphed. And so, by default, the men, drunk and uninspired, would wander to my desk, to the only person still conscious, and ask for help. The cover line for the gold-sneakered foot of Olympic athlete Michael Johnson, which read, 'No mean feet'? Mine. A cover photo of Natasha Richardson, about to play Tracy

Lord in *High Society*: 'A swell part'. Mine, too. In a big way, I liked being the small backroom girl. It was safe, relatively, as long as I didn't fax anyone. I can honestly say that at no point did I ever imagine myself as deputy editor or a feature writer proper. It was enough just to be asked to come back, day after day, and to be paid on a green casuals docket at £60 a day.

I didn't really have any skills to write about fashion, merely a sweaty-pawed desire. A red-headed American, Joyce Caruso, had been drafted in by the paper's new editor, Andrew Neil, to be deputy editor of the magazine. Of course everyone hated her. But I loved her. I loved her beauty, and her accent, and her enthusiasm. She was put in charge of the fashion supplements and I volunteered to work on these pages, given it meant working with Ralph Shandilya, a half German, half Indian photographer. Of course, he only had eyes for Joyce.

But Joyce, knowing my infatuation, engineered me a date with Ralph – a Prince concert at Wembley. There was me, Ralph, Joyce and Ian, from the art department, who was also in love with Joyce: all those hormones flying around and not one of them was after me. I wore thick, Liza Bruce black leggings and brown suede jodhpur Chelsea boots from Hobbs. But, of course, Ralph ignored me, and eventually moved in with a supermodel of his own, the liquorice-haired Susie Bick.

Back in Saffron Walden, Sue was becoming more and more house proud. She had been diverted by the boys who lived next door when we lived in London and by Peter Hammill concerts at the Commonwealth Institute in Kensington, but now there was not time for any of that. She became obsessed with cleaning the cottage. She screamed at me once when I spilled dry muesli on the kitchen floor. We had an open fire and I became more and more anxious about cleaning out the ashes the next morning. I would assemble my newspaper, brass bucket and brush, and scrabble away at the grate so it was clean before she got home from night duty. I must have had the fire going later than normal because, one morning, as I laid the ashes on the paper, it caught alight. The carpet melted. Sue was apoplectic. 'How could you be so stupid?' I had to buy a new carpet.

We had an extension built on the back of the house and a new bathroom put in upstairs, at great expense. To avoid the mess, Sue moved back home with Mum and Dad in Rettendon. I stayed behind and finally bought my horse, a stubborn, part-thoroughbred gelding called Monty I could ill afford. One weekend, I had entered a gymkhana and Mum and Dad had come to watch me compete, probably in something benign, like a bending race. The competition was running late but I remained on my horse, straight-backed, nervous, my number on my front, tied around my tiny middle. In the distance, I saw my dad look at his watch and then my parents scurried around, packing up, literally throwing things in a bag. They got in their car and disappeared, scattering those with picnics and shooting sticks. I realised it must have been 4pm, when my parents had to get home, to Get Sue Ready For Her Shift At Work. On that day of the gymkhana there was real terror in my parents' eyes. I was left alone on my horse, to compete and to finish last, unseen.

Sue often worked nights, which meant that, once she had moved back in, I had to be extra quiet. She was irrational, too. When my ancient Beetle was in the workshop, she came to pick me up from the station. 'I'm so glad you're back,' I said, leaning to kiss her on her cheek. She had been to Rettendon to get Mum to do her washing. 'You are only saying that because I am picking you up!' Driving to visit Philip and Liz (she of the posh nickname Jane) in Cambridge once, we got lost and she was screaming and swearing, refusing to stop so I could ask the way. Going round to see our parents, she punched me on the legs but, as soon as we crunched on to the drive and Dad came out with new replacement Labrador, Labby, she was as sweet as pie, laughing and giggling.

It got to the point where I was afraid to go back to Saffron Walden. I would stay in London at the office later and later and later. I would wait in my Beetle, round the corner from the cottage, until she had left for work. I started to go to Pilates classes after work, which meant I'd never get home till after 11pm. I even hired the local dance studio on the high street so I could exercise in secret, as Sue would never have let me exercise on the floor, weights strapped to ankles and arms: I might have knocked her Habitat chesterfield sofa, or woken her up. I wondered how I had ever got myself into this situation, where my life was not my own. I phoned Lyn, by now living in Australia, and told her. I was crying down the phone. 'I know,' she said. 'She used to scream at me.' Sue yelled at me one day that she knew I was taking steroids, as she had found them in my room. 'Do you have cancer?!' 'No, of course I don't have cancer.' The tablets were a leftover of the treatment I had started at the clinic. And it was these tiny tablets that were making my breasts, despite the fact I still ate very little and still exercised in any spare moment, grow bigger and bigger. I could no longer jog without holding my breasts with my arms. I hated them. I felt like a heifer, far too female.

In early 1985, we were told that a new magazine, *ELLE*, edited by Sally Brampton, who had learned her trade on *Vogue* as a fashion copy editor, was about to be launched, and a slim taster of what readers should expect was to be inserted into an edition of *The Sunday Times Magazine*. I got to work on it, and this new magazine was truly different and modern. On the very first cover was Yasmin Le Bon, looking very flat-chested, dark-haired, brown-eyed: just my type. And one of the cover lines read: 'Why French women are having breast reductions to look fashionable.' They are? Really? I read the piece, absorbing every word, taking it to heart, hugging it to my bosom. I had become more and more self-conscious about my ever-growing breasts. The rest of me was still pretty thin, so I could wear the narrow black Liza Bruce Lycra leggings, but the top half was getting bigger. I bought a baggy, grey sweater in a new boutique called, entirely coincidentally, Elle. I knew I had to do something about it.

I was 29 and I was commuting back and forth from Essex to *The Sunday Times*, worrying about my breasts. At work, I got to the point where I could not walk across the editorial floor because I was worried men were looking at my wobbly udders. I could only manage it if I held great big sheaves of proofs against me, or an encyclopaedia or a *Times World Atlas*. And so I went to see my GP.

'Yes, they are rather big,' the doctor said.

There didn't seem to be a lot of information taken down during the appointment. She took no history, didn't ask me about medication or my anorexia – she simply booked me an appointment with a surgeon. The due day came. I had taken a week off work but told no one of my plans. I parked my Beetle and went inside. I was shown to a narrow room, where I sat, waiting. I was terrified, but I knew I had to do it. Dieting had made no difference. I had to cut them off.

The surgeon came in and I took my top off. 'My goodness, they are huge,' he said. They reached almost to my waist. I could not look down at them, but stared straight ahead. He uncorked a felt-tip pen and started to draw on my breasts: big, red lines. 'You know, we have to remove the nipple, here, and move it up to here.'

I nodded, hugely embarrassed to be topless.

'And when we sew them back on, they might not take. They might turn black. This is the risk we have to take. You will also have scars here, and here. You will lose all sensation in your breasts and nipples. Does that matter?' I shook my head. 'And you will never be able to breastfeed.' I had never, ever thought I would have children. I'd barely had a period or a viable boyfriend and so breastfeeding was something I knew I'd never be able to do, like the butterfly stroke or parallel skiing

161

(I am more the permanent plough sort). He drew more lines, up under the curve of each breast.

After a fitful night, I was woken the next morning, given a sedative and walked down to the operating theatre. I remember waking up and feeling nauseous. I was swathed in bandages. I told the nurse I was going to be sick and she handed me a kidney dish. I thought about my mum in hospital in Nairobi. I missed my mum. Why had I done this to myself?

But I was pleased with the flatness of my chest, and when the surgeon came to check on my progress and unravelled the blood-soaked bandages, showing me my tiny breasts, even though they were encrusted with blood, I loved them.

'Ah, the nipples are pink,' he said, tapping them gently, 'which means they have taken.'

I was given instructions not to lift anything or sleep on my front for six months. I would have to come back to have the stitches removed; great big, black darning stitches. It all looked very crude. I got dressed that afternoon.

'Don't you have a bra?' the nurse asked me. But I didn't have one. I had had no idea what size to buy. So I went home with bandages beneath my white T-shirt. I got to the cottage and went upstairs. For the first time in years, I looked at my torso in the mirror. Blood had seeped through the T-shirt but I was amazed at my profile. I was as flat as a board.

'I look so much younger!' I said to my reflection, although no one ever noticed, or at least no one ever commented. I was not yet 30.

Chapter nine

'DON'T INTRODUCE ANY ERRORS'

I should have stayed at *The Sunday Times* but I'd been side-lined on to the London section, which was all articles about pigeons on public buildings (we published a photo of a wood pigeon on the cover once, by mistake, which had bird fanciers writing to us by the sack load) and dog fouling, so I applied for a job on the about-to-be launched *Mirabella* magazine. Owned by Rupert Murdoch, this was to be the British edition of the magazine launched by Grace Mirabella when she was fired as editor of US *Vogue*. It was for older, more intelligent women and it was a glossy, which was where I really wanted to be. Maybe this would be my fast(er) track to *Vogue*!

Lesley White, formerly of *The Face* and the best writer on *The Sunday Times*, was to be editor. Also on board were Janine di Giovanni, who would go on to make her name in the Balkans (isn't that a wonderful thing to write about some-one?), Sally Brampton, fresh from her success launching *ELLE*, the now-feminist author Natasha Walter, Ruth Picardie, who would die young of breast cancer, and Leslie Kenton. Leslie had been an idol of mine for her beauty and health articles for *Harpers & Queen*, a woman who only wore white in summer, black in winter and who had written about how she had boiled and eaten her own placenta after giving birth. The fashion editor was Caroline Baker, who I could say I had known on *The Sunday Times Magazine*, but the truth is I was too in awe of her, would not even get in a lift with her, given she had been fashion editor on *Nova*, published from 1965 to 1975, and had more or less invented punk and the New Romantics.

I got the job on *Mirabella* as chief sub, on an annual salary of £27,000 a year. It was 1990. I had to appoint my team. I hired a deputy called Sally Jones, an American girl with ter-rible skin. And I called Central Saint Martins College to see if there were any graduates looking for a job. A young man called Jeremy Langmead answered the telephone. 'Yes, I am,' he said eagerly.

I met him at a café next to *The Sunday Times* office. He was wearing tweeds and was handsome in a *Brideshead Revisited* sort of way. He had done the fashion journalism degree course and brought with him his magazine for men called *Bob*. I liked him immediately and offered him the job. On his first day, he sat next to me, as eager and brown-eyed as a beaver cub. I told him the first rule of subbing was 'not to introduce any errors'. On our second day, I arrived at my desk and there was a very beautiful young woman called India Knight sitting opposite me. Her black hair was scraped back in a tight knot, and she wore large, gold, hooped earrings. I thought she was Spanish but it turned out she was half Pakistani, half Belgian. I went straight to Lesley's office to demand who on earth she was. 'She is the daughter of Andrew Knight, chairman of News International, so we have to give her a job. She has no experience but she has a degree from Cambridge.'

Hmmm. I wanted to snub India from that moment on, but she was so likeable and funny, I found I couldn't. She soon wrote all our captions, as she had a gift with words, and a good sense of humour. Despite her rich parents and gorgeous loft in Hampstead, she was always broke, so the routine soon became that, come six o'clock, we would leave the offices on the Haymarket and go to a pub called the Blue Posts on Rupert Street, or to a narrow members-only drinking club near Soho Square, owned by a Belgian, where India ran up a huge tab. He went on to found Belgo, a chain of restaurants selling mussels, so perhaps India paid him back. She would always stand at a cashpoint, willing it to give her money, for all the world as though it were a slot machine, subject to luck.

Also on staff were Tamara Yeardye, who would go on, as Tamara Mellon, to take over and relaunch Jimmy Choo, and Alisa Green, who would marry Stephen Marks, founder of French Connection. But, for now, we were all struggling with a new magazine. With a great deal of foresight, Lesley started putting celebrities on the cover: Ali MacGraw and Joely Richardson, who unfortunately was photographed sitting on a chair, elbows on knees, to all intents and purposes as though she were on the toilet. Inside we had columnists, but they were hugely intellectual, including Edward Said. Sally Brampton wrote a piece on the rise of plastic surgery in Brazil, and interviewed another cover star, Sindy Crawford. The fashion was wonderful, as was the beauty copy, but it was all very upmarket.

Working on the magazine was fun. I didn't write anything for it, but Jeremy was as keen as mustard. He would turn up early every morning, sit up straight, eager for anything you could throw at him. He wrote a small piece for the News section in the middle and he, too, had it laminated, encircling his desk with his show cards. He later became editor of *Esquire* and was best man at my wedding, while India gave a reading.

While I was at *Mirabella*, I went to a new jazz club in Lewisham, south London, with Beverley D'Silva, whom I'd hired as a casual sub to help out. Bev was a beautiful Sri-Lankan-born woman, a little older than me, who had started to make her name on magazines. She was in love with a German photographer called Christian Bader, who used to stand up and go to bed in the middle of her squashed dinner parties. That night, I met a handsome squaddie at the club. He took my phone number at work – I wouldn't dare give him my home number and risk Sue talking to him – and the next day he phoned me up. We arranged to go on a date to see a film. I met him after work at the Blue Posts, off Leicester

Square, probably with India et al. looking on, waiting to see if I was okay. When he turned up, in a suit and big black over-coat, I didn't recognise him, which wasn't a good sign. He was very on edge, a state I discovered was quite normal for him. We had a drink, then walked to Leicester Square to see *Teenage Mutant Ninja Turtles*. I refused a lift to the station, and that was that.

I didn't tell Sue about my date, knowing she would not approve. It's strange, given she was so much wilder than me in her schooldays, what with Steve and Blackie, that she became so fond of being on the disapproving moral high ground.

In all the years I'd worked in London, I had not had a sniff of a boyfriend. I had had one snog, from a young photogra-pher, who I'd met at *The Sunday Times Magazine* Christmas party, 1989, held at the RCA galleries on The Mall. He was wearing a woollen sweater and asked me to leave the party with him. I couldn't believe my luck. I'd seen him bring film into the office, always clad in tight cycling shorts. He was blond and improbably handsome. So we left the party, and when I touched his woolly by mistake (no! not his willy!) I noticed it was hard. Wow. So this is what a man's chest feels like. The wool was wet, as he'd been spilling beer down his front. We walked along The Mall, then went for a vegan curry. I was too excited to eat, of course: some people feed butter-flies, I starve them. He told me he had a girlfriend and that I had 'movie star teeth'. I still wasn't sure what on earth he was doing with me (I realise now it was just because he was drunk). We left the restaurant and walked around Trafalgar Square and he kissed me, right outside the National Portrait Gallery. It was the best kiss of my life. Still is. I blush when I round that corner in a cab. I told him I had to catch the bus on the Strand to Liverpool Street, to catch the last train home. 'I'll come with you,' he said. But I knew this was not possible. Sue.

'No,' I said, spotting a number 9 bus, breaking into a run. 'You can't.'

I was in love with him from that moment. I was in a daze on the journey home, stopping at Journey's Friend for my vat of black coffee, which I always drank on my way home to keep me from falling asleep and missing my station. That weekend, mindful of the Montgenèvre debacle, I bought K-Y Jelly in Boots, then had the problem of where to hide it from Sue. I went to work early on Monday, convinced my new obsession would come into the office and speak to me. Finally, I would have a boyfriend and lose my virginity. But several weeks went by, and nothing. And then I spotted him, with his messenger bag, and fluorescent legs. But he just ignored me. He didn't speak to me again until, about 10 years later, at a work party in Hoxton Square. He said, 'Liz, right?' I nodded. 'Didn't you get married and have, like, three children?' 'No!' I shouted. 'God, no!' And in my head I said, 'No, because I was waiting for you to call me!' 'Oh, must have been the other Liz in the office. I thought it was you.'

I still wonder who misinformed him. Who ruined my chance of happiness?

For my second date with The Squaddie I wore a black Azzedine Alaïa jacket, bought at huge expense from Browns, Levi's and a Donna Karan black wool body (I have a long trunk, like a dachshund, so it was vastly uncomfortable: who on earth would put poppers in such a place?). He picked me up from the office on the Haymarket. He drove an old BMW and had a Vodafone car phone, something I'd never come across before. He gave me his car phone number. Even to this day, if I ever call someone and get the message, 'The Vodafone you are calling is switched off', I start to sweat, feeling a strange disappointment in my groin area.

We sped back to the jazz club, where we sat on stools at the bar. This is the life, I thought to myself. I am wearing Alaïa, in a jazz club in a particularly dangerous part of London, with a tall, handsome man. He drank a lot of Stolichnaya vodka. A screen above the bar was showing the Seal video, 'Crazy'. 'Like Seal, do you?' he said, the first hint of jealousy. He told me he had been married to a Russian model and had a daughter. He then suggested we drive to his flat to meet his brother. 'Okay,' I said. We drove recklessly down endless Victorian terraced streets. We stopped outside a small terraced house and he unlocked a door. It led straight into a steep flight of steps, to a flat upstairs. It was like a slum – clothes on every radiator, a disgusting bathroom, a kitchen full of unwashed cups and plates. He was nervous. His brother was in the front room watching a horror film. Wordlessly, we joined him. I became more and more terrified, but not because of the film. I was a very long way from home.

Finally, at about 1am, he led me into the bedroom, which could just about fit a double bed. I sat on it. He closed the door. It was pitch black.

'Why has he left me on my own in this bedroom?' I thought. 'Is this where I'm going to sleep? Well, he could have said good night!' And then a pair of pillowy cool lips were on mine, and I was pushed backwards on to the bed. Oh, so he was still in the room. Only I could go back to a man's house, be shown into his bedroom and assume he had found me so repulsive that at the last minute he had gone to sleep elsewhere.

He undressed me. I was rigid, fearful of a repeat performance of what happened with Albert. I had not had the foresight to pack the K-Y Jelly bought for my previous encounter, which was buried in a field back in Essex in case my sister discovered it on one of her marathon cleaning sessions. But The Squaddie was so forceful, he entered in one. 'Ow!' I cried, dazed from the pain. He banged away at me for hours, sweating profusely, showering me with moisture. I received no sexual satisfaction at all, merely experienced rigid fear and discomfort, especially as a packet of Tuc biscuits was in his unmade, nylon-sheeted bed. Eventually, he opened a window and I stuck my head out of it.

In the morning, a Saturday, we awoke to the sight of badly bloodstained sheets. 'Why didn't you tell me you were having your period? God, that is disgusting,' he said, not thinking for a second that, aged 32 (although I told him I was 26), I was still a virgin, despite the fingering from the mad professor. He asked about the scars on my breasts, too. I told him I had had a couple of suspicious lumps removed. How much better that seemed to me than the truth.

I had told Sue I was staying with Bev and had arranged to meet her in the lobby of Heal's on Tottenham Court Road as she wanted to go shopping, then get her hair done in Covent Garden. Terrified I would be late, I gulped down a black coffee and walked to the station. It was snowing and so I had to run the last mile or so. I got to the shop, only to find Sue was late, too. I stood there for two hours, waiting, nursing my terrible, dirty secret.

We carried on going out. Me travelling back and forth to Saffron Walden, working on *Mirabella*, and going for dates. I introduced my new man to my friends at a party on Old Street one night. India later told me he had tried to sell her drugs. We went out one night with Bev and offered to give her a lift home to nearby Blackheath. On the way, a taxi driver cut us up. The Squaddie swore and started to chase the taxi through the suburban streets. Bev became terrified and angry, and told him to slow down for imaginary childhood pony's sake. He took no notice. The taxi pulled over and the couple in the back got out. As they did so, The Squaddie slammed on the brakes and got out, leaving the driver's door open and us wailing in the back, helpless. He marched up to the driver's window, like someone out of a Western, pulled the taxi driver out of the cab and proceeded to use him as a punchbag on the floor. The couple looked on, horrified, and they pleaded with us, by now screaming at him to stop, to do something.

He dropped the driver, walked back to the car, got in, and we drove off. He dropped Bev at her flat and she got out. 'Are you coming with me?' she asked, pleading.

'No, I will go back with him,' I said, barely able to look her in the eye.

The next day, she confronted me at work. 'You are not going to see him again, are you?' she asked me.

'No, of course not.' That day, he sent red roses and a card that read, 'Can't send you black coffee, can I?'

That night he was parked by the entrance to King's House, on the Haymarket. I got in. We had sex in a car park near the Elephant & Castle. We had a lot of sex outdoors. He never once brought me to orgasm. Once, he just drove to a Sainsbury's, parked and imaginary childhood ponied me over the boot. I didn't much like him and he was now known as The Mad One among my colleagues at *Mirabella* (he was, indeed, mad: in a restaurant, he would always sit facing the door, in case of terrorists entering to pick up a vegetarian Indian takeaway. At these wretched meals, he would tell me not to slump my head into my neck, giving myself a double chin), but he was a boyfriend, something I had never known before.

I took him home to Saffron Walden, just the once. It was late. Sue was in bed at the top of the house. The Squaddie seemed overly large in the tiny house, clumsy. He slid on his socks on the bathroom floor and nearly crashed out the window. 'They could have arrested me for breaking and exiting,' he said loudly (I kept trying to shush him), the first and last funny thing he ever said to me. The next morning, Sue had already gone to work. We got up and drove back up the M11. That evening, exhausted, I got home. Sue confronted me about bringing The Squaddie back for the night and flew into a rage.

The next day, I left the house with my duvet and nothing else – I couldn't live there any longer. I was now homeless. I called my friend Bridget, who had gone to live in Spain to work for *Hola!* She said I could rent her flat, a tiny attic at the top of a house in Finsbury Park, near the tube, and on the number 19 bus route. That night, after work, with my duvet under one arm, I stopped off at M&S at The Angel, and bought a roll, a tub of salad, some coffee, and a knife and a fork. I caught the bus to my new life – living on my own. I had no telly and only Bridget's awful sofa and bed. But I was happy. I was free at last.

But there was more bad news. One night, at The Squaddie's flat (he was out, having one of his interminable haircuts), there was a knock at the door. I went down the steep stairs to answer it. There were two policemen. 'We have a warrant for the arrest of . . .' 'He's not here.' 'When will he be back?' 'I have no idea.' 'Well, please make sure he gets this summons.' I took it and crept upstairs. I steamed it open. It was a summons for his trial for assaulting his ex-wife. I sealed it up and left it on the side. We never spoke of it. That was the end.

Well, almost the end.

He moved in with me to Bridget's flat but, one night, I threw all his clothes out of the window, on to the ground. He had driven me one too many times at top speed, having downed one too many bottles of Stoly.

At work, the morning after the clothes eviction when I had imagined I was in a dreadful romantic comedy, we were called to a meeting. The magazine was going to be closed, after just ten issues. I was called to the managing editor's office, a woman called Liz Rees-Jones. I was told I would get one month's pay. That was it. I decided to use it as a deposit on a flat of my own. Sue was still in the house in Saffron Walden, so I had to get ANOTHER mortgage. Jeremy, who went straight to work for ELLE DECOR and was by now engaged to India (which we all thought rather odd, as he seemed clearly homosexual), helped me look. I finally found a ground-floor, one-bedroom flat on Haberdasher Street, a treeless road, with a housing estate at one end and a cheap liquor store at the other, near Old Street tube. It was £80,000.

I decided, encouraged by the merchandise editor of *Mirabella*, an immaculate German called Claudine, to get a cat. I went one Saturday in the Beetle to the house of a fashion designer friend of Jeremy's called Simon, whose cat, Domino, had had a litter of kittens on his bed. One was called Snoopy, a tabby with smart white paws. I took him home. It was to be the love of my life.

I still had to earn some money, though. I freelanced for a day or so on a women's health magazine, imaginatively called *Women's Health*. I spent one day subbing on *Marie Claire*, whose offices were then based in Knightsbridge. And I called the chief sub of *The Sunday Times*, to see if I could get any shifts there. I went for the interview, at the warehouse in

Wapping, in east London. The chief sub was called Caroline and she offered me some work. There was no permanency, no sick pay, no holiday pay. I would turn up each day, working on Culture and the Look page, which was the one broadsheet page of fashion. Occasionally, the writers would swan in, usually on a Friday. There was Helen Fielding, later to write *Bridget Jones*, and Polly Samson, who would marry Dave Gilmour. Helen would sit on the desk of Harry Ritchie, the literary editor, and laugh and gossip. They went out and about, and reported on parties: they certainly weren't stuck in a flea- and TB-ridden, leaky warehouse that served as our offices. Kate Carr, whom I'd first met on *Company*, an earnest, red-headed girl with long skirts that invariably got tucked in her knickers, was on the Look desk. She had leapfrogged me spectacularly.

As a sub I had a new-fangled computer, which had a small, black screen on which you typed in bright green letters. I learned how to translate type on to a page, using all sorts of elaborate codes, something I could never do now: I've actually lost skills, not gained them. I can no longer even rustle up 'cheesy potatoes', the only dish I mastered at school.

As each page was ready, we would go down to the composing room, where printers pasted each proof on to card and propped them around the room. I would then type the captions and take the proofs upstairs to deliver them beneath the doors of all the editors, who had long since gone home. All the print workers from Fleet Street had been sacked and it was still hairy going into Wapping each day, braving the men with banners. Our cars would be searched underneath, and the whole place was surrounded with barbed wire. To earn extra money, I would do overtime, earning £20 or so for every extra hour. I tried to work until 3am each night: I only managed to feed Snoopy with a battery-operated dish, which would open, making him jump, at certain times of the day.

There were many people in the warehouse, on the arts pages, who had been there for what seemed like centuries. There was Barbara, the myopic puzzles editor, who refused to be parted from her equally ancient typewriter. There was Graeme, the gardening editor. Dilys Powell filed her film reviews from some far-off place and her typewriter was so old, we often had to guess at the words. Her copy always had great big holes, where she had bashed with frustration, or a key was missing.

The writers on the Culture section were the worst: Paul Driver would complain to the editor if you changed a single word. When you edited a piece, you had to put any changes or cuts in notes, which showed up as pale green and didn't come out on the proof, but it meant the editors could see what you had done to the copy, should Paul complain and want a moratorium on why a semicolon had been changed to a full one.

The hours were so long and arduous that people would often keel over at their desks. I could not afford food, which suited me fine as I was still determined to be thin, and so I took cornflakes in each day, which was all I had to eat: there was free milk in the canteen. For the first time in my life I was ahead.

My second break came when it was decided to launch a TV section, to coincide with the launch of the Sky channels, also owned by Murdoch. I was given a full-time job on this section, at £30,000 a year. I was able to write: two line haikus, the film listings for the Sky movie channels. They became more and more surreal and obscure. 'Cary Grant turns gay all of a sudden, while a Big Cat runs amok' (*Bringing Up Baby*). And 'Glenn Close proves she is not a vegetarian, and has a really bad perm' (*Fatal Attraction*). I had to check all the TV listings and the regional variations. After a few years, I was made deputy chief sub of Culture, the new broadsheet Style section and the TV guide. There was no home life, no social life. I spent each weekend dragging my washing to the launderette. There were no windows in the warehouse offices, merely fluorescent strip lighting: I don't think they wanted us to be distracted. I was very glad to be summoned back to *The Sunday Times Magazine*, located on the other side of the dual carriageway. Kate Carr was now editor and, when she arrived, she was aghast at the waste, the lack of hard work, the over-population. When she asked how long it would take to get some copy on proof, she was told, 'Maybe a month.' She culled more or less everybody.

We were now being taught to work on Apple Macs: small, grey machines. Gone, almost overnight, were the typesetters. Instead, for the first time, copy was emailed in, to the one central email address. We were taught to click on boxes and create picture boxes, and style type. Overnight, we could write an A matter and fiddle with it on screen to get it right. We still didn't use the internet, though. We had a great big reference library and we would phone the librarians to ask for a spelling or date of birth. Often, we would have to go and get out the 'cuts': yellowing clippings, dated and folded meticulously. At the end of the day, these folders would be collected in wicker baskets and taken back to the library.

Zoë Heller was hired as a new columnist, at the front of the magazine, writing about her life as a single woman having moved to New York. I was always in awe of Zoë, who was terribly nice. She would type her column, walk to Kinko's, fax it to us in the office, and then I would type it into the system. But then Kate Carr was ousted. One day, a man called Robin Morgan just turned up, and sat at a desk. She was undermined and, although she put up a fight, she soon left and Robin took her place. She later died of breast cancer, leaving a husband and small children, citing the extreme stress she was put under as the cause of her disease.

In 1991, not long after rejoining the *Magazine*, compiling a part-work called 'Makers of the Twentieth Century', I met Useless Boyfriend Number Two, who turned out to be only slightly less mad than The Squaddie. I had been invited to the launch of a new album by Omar ('There's Nothing Like This!'), and he was on the door. He had his own PR firm, called The Watchmen, based on Old Street. The next day, he rang me up, asking why I had left the launch almost straight away. I told him I'd had to go to the album launch of Massive

Attack; they'd just changed their name to Massive because of the Gulf War. He asked if I could go to his offices, where he could show me his clients' portfolios. Again, I mistook work for attraction.

Well, I was very excited. I dismissed the fact he was probably only interested in me because he was a PR and I worked on a national newspaper. I dressed carefully – a cream Nicole Farhi cardigan – and drove the quarter mile from my Old Street flat, which I hadn't even been able to afford to furnish with a sofa yet, just those few bits and pieces I'd taken to Bridget's, to his offices on Eagle Wharf Road. I parked the car and spent some time checking my make-up in a tiny mirror, wielding tweezers and an eyelash comb (I only ever look at my face in tiny, bite-size sections). I went inside. As I entered his office, I noticed his window directly overlooked my car, so he had clearly seen me adjusting and fiddling, which put me at a distinct disadvantage.

I told him I might be able to get him styling work on *The Sunday Times*, which is what he really wanted to do (again, perhaps gay alarm bells should have gone off), and his eyes lit up. He was a strange-looking young man, 26 years old, with a huge nose and a flat top. He said, being Jamaican, he encountered a lot of racism; people yelled 'Pasadenas' at him in the road. I'd have thought this was a compliment. He wore navy, well-pressed (hence shiny) trousers high on his waist, and a fine-knit Smedley sweater. I hate to admit it but I think my taste had been swayed by the video for Soul II Soul's 'Back to Life' video: I wanted to be the thin, young woman with a sweet face, gyrating in the background wearing a headscarf. I wanted to go out with a member of Jodeci, or one of the Tonys in Tony! Toni! Toné!

He called my flat that weekend, asking if I wanted to go and see the new Woody Allen film. I said okay. Nothing happened. No kiss. No nothing. He then asked me out for a drink, so I met him at a bar. I was late and I could tell he was annoyed. He was very serious, and seriously into hip-hop and acid jazz: I'd forgotten about the Brand New Heavies and The Young Disciples. On the night of our first kiss Useless Boyfriend Number Two moved in, thinking it far too late to get the tube home to Ealing and his parents' house. My main function, I discovered as we dated, was to procure him free hip-hop CDs, which involved a very close and duplicitous relationship with all the major record label PRs. I also had to tape *Yo! MTV Raps* each night at work at Wapping, the only place that seemed to have Sky. And thus I was introduced to Ice Cube and Eric B. & Rakim and Public Enemy. He also had videotapes by a preacher called Louis Farrakhan.

The strange thing is, I realise now but didn't then, that I was a bit of a catch, given I would always get home from Wapping laden with M&S ready meals. At least, I was relatively normal. Well, okay, I was still young. I had stabilised my eating, having had the breast reduction and been able to afford my own in-house step machine. The cornflakes-only diet was due to financial straits, not purely anorexia: I got into debt to feed my new boyfriend. And, although he was kind, he didn't have a lot going for him. He seemed to have no money, and never contributed to household bills. I remember once, in my ancient Beetle on Upper Street, we stopped for a Domino's Pizza. He waited in the car while I went in to get it. I saw he had £20 in his wallet. But still he let me pay.

I was spending a lot, it has to be said, on clothes. I had discovered Jones, a his and hers boutique on Floral Street in Covent Garden. There I bought a navy Comme des Garçons pleated skirt, and an ivory Dries van Noten raincoat I wore at all times of year, indoors and out. I bought a green men's blazer from Jeremy, and a gold Jasper Conran waistcoat that made me look like a circus performer when teamed with the olive Calvin Klein silk shorts. I had a blue quilted parka and black T-shirt from Katharine Hamnett on Sloane Street. I bought a petrol blue heavy crepe skirt from Alaïa that was far too big, and which I eventually gifted to India. But none of this seemed to impress Useless Boyfriend Number Two. My big admission is that, for about the first year we lived together, he refused to have sex with me, even though we slept in the same bed and I paid for everything.

But eventually he gave in and started to sleep with me, carefully using a condom. I would sneak into my tiny bathroom after sex, empty it out, and put it inside me. (I much later wrote about this deception in the *Daily Mail*, prompting *The New Yorker* to nickname me Jiz Loans.) I wanted to keep this man. I wanted a coffee-coloured baby. We would go to the Jazz Café in Camden, but he'd always make sure he was a few paces ahead, or a few paces behind, so we didn't appear to be together: I was Prince Philip to his Queen Elizabeth. At home, he spent all his time sat on a speaker in his ironed trousers, making mixed tapes, or trying to identify samples used in hip-hop records. Was it Rufus and Chaka Khan? I pretended to care. He was the PR for a London soul singer called Des'ree, who once wrote the immortal lyric, 'Lucky rabbit's tail' instead of foot. How cruel, either way. I persuaded him to use a photographer called Marcus Tomlinson for her album cover, a favourite at *The Sunday Times Magazine* and who had shot many black music stars, and so I just assumed he was also black. He was enthusiastic and in a meeting with Des'ree's record company executives, fought long and hard for a 'brother' to shoot a fellow black artist. They caved. The cover shoot day dawned. Marcus turned up, and was 100 per cent white. I think he might even have been Scandinavian. I received a furious phone call. 'Who did you think he was, Michael Jackson?'

I got him that styling job in *The Sunday Times Magazine*, though. In a special issue all about hip-hop, he styled a fashion shoot showing all the different types of black street fashion, from string vests, to low-slung, Kriss Kross jeans. This didn't make him like me any more deeply or follow me more meekly, given he eventually ran off with a fashion PR called Jenny, who was black, of course she was.

I heard from his former colleague that Useless Boyfriend Number Two had travelled to Africa, where he was told there was a curse on his head. He came back and didn't work for two years. But I sometimes remember him and his high-waisted trousers, his TCP for aftershave (he was obsessed with never having razor bumps), and I wonder if I was responsible, in part, for his demise. A mystic told me that one of the men I had dated was gay. And I think Useless Boyfriend Number Two might have been, hence the angst, the reluctance, the lack of engagement. But maybe not. Maybe he just didn't fancy me.

Was I only ever interested in black men? An early triumph was when I had phoned up *Interview* magazine and suggested an interview with Seal. They said yes. I duly interviewed him and he even phoned my mum's house once, asking for me. But the truth is, no white man ever wanted me, or asked me out.

My break-up with this second boyfriend was slow and painful. When he finally decided he had to move out, to temporarily sleep in his office, which was now in Ovington Square in Knightsbridge (he had a rich male friend), I offered to take all his stuff in my Beetle. It was mainly acid jazz CDs, anyway, and over-pressed clothes. We drove west from Old Street and, as I negotiated the roundabout at Marble Arch, he told me he was 'seeing' Jenny. I nearly crashed the car. But still, I unloaded him, helping carry his stuff down to the basement. Today, the new, angry me would have just pulled over outside Pizza Express and dumped all his rubbish on the roadside. When I finally got back to my empty flat, I sat by my hi-fi and played Prince's 'Adore', over and over again. He had left me a message on my answer machine (isn't it a shame these clunky machines no longer exist? It was always a warm, sometimes blinking presence to come home to), 'Liz. I just wanted to phone and say thank you for helping me so much. I really do love you, and I want you to know I will always be here for you as a friend.'

That was 1995. I never heard from him again. Ooh. Once. Three years later, when I was editor of *Marie Claire*, my assistant Kerry Smith put through a phone call from, 'He says he knows you?' I picked up the phone. 'Hi, Liz. I hope you haven't let success change you. I wondered if you could help me get a pair of cut-price plane tickets to Jamaica?'

I never helped him with those plane tickets. I wish I'd been that careful with the people who were about to enter my life.

Chapter ten

'Victoria Beckham, Ooo eeez she?'

Nineteen-ninety-seven was a horrible year. I woke up on Sunday morning, on 31 August, to see on the news that Princess Diana had been killed in Paris. I immediately drove to work, helping to piece together the inevitable tribute supplements about her life in fashion. The funeral was like a dress rehearsal for my dad's. He was now diagnosed with cancer.

He was ashamed to be ill. He said to my mum, 'Tell the little girls I am sorry.' He was in and out of Addenbrooke's Hospital, where I would ferry my mum, who never did learn to drive, to visit him. For the first time, he said to my mum, 'Doesn't Lizzie look nice in her trousers?' He had never commented on my appearance before. I once took my brother Nick, too. He wandered off, as he is wont to do, and I had to page him. 'What does your little brother look like?' said the woman on reception, imagining a toddler. 'He's about forty-five. Tell people to be on the lookout for someone in Seventies clothing and Cuban heels.' He was not best pleased.

I was still at *The Sunday Times*, now working on the new Style section. It was thought that there were enough lifestyle topics to warrant an entirely separate magazine, although for the first few issues, months, even, we had no idea what to put in it. Jeremy was now my boss. One of his first acts as Style Supremo, as he liked to be called, was to hire Isabella Blow as fashion director.

You knew Isabella had arrived in the office, which she did rarely, as the Wapping compound was far too ugly, when the scent of tuberose wafted up into the air conditioning. All the men on the paper were terrified of her, in her hats and strange costumes, a fact I rather enjoyed. And while she was clearly talented, she was uncontrollable when it came to budgets. She once went on a complicated shoot in Russia, which cost thousands, and shot the clothes entirely indoors, against a grey wall.

Sue and I were back in touch again. She would visit me in London and we would go shopping in the Conran Shop. She had started seeing someone – Robert, whom she met when she went into his antiques shop in Essex to buy yet another pine cupboard. She became pregnant and seemed on more of an even keel.

And then, in 1998, my dad died. Mum had slept in the double bed every night since he came home, not caring about his coughing or the fact he would cry out with pain. It was a Saturday and, hearing he was fading, having received another dose of morphine that would probably finish him off, I drove as fast as I could in my ancient Beetle, which, like my dad's Hillman, you also had to double declutch. But I got there too late. So much for reliable German engineering. 'He's gone,' said Tony, who had been summoned from Edinburgh and was now crumpled at the back door, the red faded to rosé. Nick was at the dining-room table, rolling a cigarette. My mum was slumped on her worn and bald three-piece suite, broken. I couldn't go and see the body upstairs. Sue had only just had a baby and was nearly hysterical.

On the day of the funeral, I got in the limo with my mum, who said, as she held my hand, 'I can't believe my darling is in that box.' Clare was unable to cope, staggering at the edge of the grave. Tony's wife, Laura, was drinking by this time. A shy young woman, she had started to drink to make herself more sociable. She soon lost her job as a teacher, and her two daughters would get home to find her on the floor, an empty bottle by her side. When she died, she was found on her own in her flat, surrounded by pizza boxes, their contents intact. She would order a pizza and a bottle of wine, a pizza and a bottle of wine.

For whatever the reason, Clare appeared to be on a path of self-destruction. She eventually got divorced, spent the money from the sale of the family home on an old Jaguar car, and now lives in assisted housing, alone, penniless, while even her sons see little of her. She keeps breaking bones and ending up in hospital. She is there now, as I type. I ask myself, where are the men now that she needs them? Lyn, too, having given up her job as a nurse on arrival in Australia to be a mum, has only her pension. When she first moved to London to work at the National Heart Hospital, living in a nursing home on Westmoreland Street, I used to laugh at her because she only ever knew her way to Debenhams on Oxford Street. Men adored her dotty nature, her reliance on them. But where are they now? My mum was never liberated: she only ever sipped slowly on a glass of Bristol Cream at Christmas; it tended to evaporate faster than she could drink it. But a whole generation of women who let their hair down in the Sixties are now reaching pension age alone with the bottle half empty.

I don't know how my mum survived losing a man she had spent every single night with since 1945, bar hospital stays for the rigors and the neck stretching. When my mum became housebound with arthritis, unable to do any shopping, my dad, who was too ill with the beginnings of cancer to drive, would walk to the shops. And my mum, holding on to the curtains to keep herself upright, would wait by the window the entire time he was gone, until he turned the corner, still with that old army gait. And he would stop, and give her a jaunty salute, and she would blush.

In the summer of 1998, I hired a villa in Italy, meaning to treat my mum. I got there a week early, to make sure there was food and to hire a car. Sue, her new baby Joe and Mum flew out and I picked them up from the airport at Pisa. I'd hired a cot for Joe but, of course, he slept in Sue's bed and screamed if you dipped him in the pool, which was freezing. I hired a cook to make us risotto and creamy tiramisu, which I pushed around the plate with a spoon: my default setting when under duress is to stop eating. One day, we drove to San Gimignano. Mum pushed Joe's pram, mainly because she was too crippled and stiff to walk unaided. Arriving in the beautiful medieval square to get ice cream, Sue noticed Mum had pushed the pram through some dog poo. She literally went mad. 'How will I ever get it off?!'

But then, over the next year or so, Mum deteriorated. She needed carers, at first once a day, then twice, then three times a day. 'Hello, dear,' she would say to a selection of well-meaning Eastern Europeans. 'I'm fine. I'm getting better.' Which of course she wasn't.

In 1998, I applied to be editor of *Marie Claire*. I sent off my portfolio – various cover shoots I had set up with Geri Halliwell, Emma Bunton and David Beckham, and of course the famous and memorable 'pop quiz'. I was interviewed by the publisher, Rita Lewis. I was interviewed again. I had no hope in hell of being chosen and so, when I was rung while at my desk at Style, I was shocked. Then I turned the job down.

'What is it? Is the seventy thousand pounds not enough, the company car? We could look again at the package.'

But it wasn't the package. It was the fact I had knocked

three years off my age when writing my CV – I was now 40 – and couldn't possibly accept the job, as I would be found out. How could I have been so stupid? My defence is that I felt I had not achieved enough by this stage, but it was still stupid: this was my dream job and I had ruined everything.

So, I wrote Rita a letter, telling her I had excised three years off my age. To give her huge credit, she called me and said, 'It's not as if you are a hundred! Of course I still want you!'

Everyone at *The Sunday Times* was shocked. (I was now ghosting a column by Meg Mathews, writing her jokes, which she never got. She would speed into town from her mansion in the countryside in her Porsche Boxster to drop off photos to accompany the column. One was a photo of a dog she'd rescued in Camden; she insisted we print a black stripe over his face, in case his old owner, a drug dealer, recognised him and wanted him back.) The editor, by now John Witherow, called me into his office and said, 'Producing a standalone cover that has to sell on the newsstand is a very different thing to what you do now.'

Never a truer word was spoken.

Right from the word go, the job was a stressful nightmare, despite the copious amounts of St John's wort I poured down my throat. Looking back, I realise I was never assertive enough, never put my foot down, never trusted my instincts, as I was always terrified I wasn't good enough, that my appointment was a mistake, a fluke.

Marie Claire had been launched in the UK by Glenda Bailey, who had managed to close *Honey*, owned by the same company, IPC. She had done a terrific job with this new format, coming up with a magazine that mixed high fashion with stories on women's struggles around the world. She had left the magazine to edit the American version and Juliet Warkentin had taken over. In 1998, the magazine sold 600,000 copies in the UK with its 10th birthday issue.

I didn't know it when I started on the magazine, but this high peak, due mostly to money-off vouchers, made my job very difficult. My sales would necessarily be lower. I made so many mistakes as editor, I don't really know where to start.

The biggest error was that I wanted to be liked. There were two women on the magazine who had been there since the beginning and who hated me, and hated change. I should have said from the outset I wanted my own team. Even when another magazine folded, the company insisted I interview a sacked deputy editor to be my new deputy, and when I said I didn't think she was good enough, she took me to a tribunal! The two women did eventually leave, with a huge payoff, and promptly launched a rival publication: an exclusion period should have been written into the severance deal.

My first day was horrendous. I wore a new, brown Jil Sander trouser suit over a T-shirt, and a pair of flat slides: the early precursor to Havaiana flip-flops. I had only met two members of staff before my first day: Kerry Smith, the editor's PA, whom I immediately liked for her cool, unflappable demeanour and intelligence; and Sarah Walter, the fashion director, who seemed organised and well connected.

On that first day, I must have seemed the boss from hell. I was staggered that all the young women seemed so ill informed, and slow, and lazy. Coming from newspapers, where you get to your desk, having vacuumed all the other papers, and immediately log on and start typing, I was unused to women sitting around chatting, sipping coffee. They never seemed to have read anything in the news, wrapped up, as they were, in their own safe worlds. Like me, I suppose, at *Company*, when I had never given a thought to sales, or budgets, or the stress Maggie Goodman must have been under. My mantra nevertheless soon became, 'Face the front!'

And the tears! I wanted my features team all in one place, so asked the ancient executive fashion editor to move her desk. Oh, dear. You'd have thought I'd euthanised her even more ancient mother. I had to deal with maternity leaves, demands for pay, demands to take a sabbatical, and disgruntled subs telling their stories to the *Guardian*. (The most ludicrous story about me while I was an editor was in the *Daily Telegraph*. They wrote I had gone home in the middle of the day when there was due a total eclipse of the sun to cover my cats' eyes – I had by now got another cat, Squeaky, a black, overweight dominatrix – lest they look up and be blinded. This was nonsense. I went home and fed each of them biscuits, so they would be looking down, at their bowls, instead of up.) I'd secured, with the help of a writer called Kate Thornton, a cover for Christmas 1999 featuring the three female stars of *Friends*: Jennifer Aniston, Courteney Cox and Lisa Kudrow. This was an enormous coup at the time and my publisher phoned me up to congratulate me. When a sub cut the copy without asking my permission, I became angry. I was in New York with Kerry, meeting agents to try to persuade them to give us access to their stars for our cover, when I heard the *Guardian* was going to run an exposé on how horrible I was. It was a lesson: stick your neck out, work hard, succeed, and you will be crucified.

The New York and West Coast agents representing the stars we needed for our covers were terrifying. Kerry and I were frequently taken aback by their demands and their rudeness. Talking to Renée Zellweger's agent, she said she would not have her interviewed by my new star writer, Emma Forrest, as Emma had written of Sarah Michelle Gellar, another actress in her stable, 'Her voice is as thin as her West Coast body.'

I discovered that working for *Marie Claire* was not the same as working for *Vogue*. We could not secure the top tier of models, as they all wanted to hold out for *Vogue*. If they were shot by us first, *Vogue* wouldn't touch them, wanting to launch the careers of new girls themselves. The top photographers would not work for us, either. Only Patrick Demarchelier agreed to shoot our covers, for a fee of about £20,000 a day. I flew to Los Angeles for one important shoot with Geri Halliwell, staying in the Mondrian hotel, all white walls, white, slatted blinds and bronzed, Nicole-Farhi-clad bellhops. We arrived at the studio, having first been faxed Geri's list of dietary requirements: brown rice and vegetables, and a latte with 1 per cent fat milk. (Only Puff Daddy was more high maintenance, requiring two people to hold his mobile phones to his ears, and a full-length mirror on set, so he could check his pose before he was snapped.)

Despite her success with the Spice Girls, Demarchelier had clearly never heard of Halliwell. The stylist had hung up several rails of clothes: these young women tend to have a scatter-gun approach, calling in as many garments as humanly possible, in the hope something will suit. Geri stripped to her knickers in front of everyone and revealed herself as having the body of a child. We ended up putting her in one of her own T-shirts and a pair of faded Levi's. I thought she looked cool and sexy and undone, but this, too, was a big mistake, as I would find out to my cost.

The cover is the prime advertising slot for the high fashion brands who buy space inside. I should never have wasted a cover by not featuring a high end designer. A designer who books space expects editorial coverage in direct relation to how much they spend in the magazine. I once received an irate fax from Giorgio Armani's PR (his whole team seemed perpetually in fear of the tanned, silver-backed one; one of his key PR's hair fell out with the stress), telling me they wanted a cover and on a star they deemed suitably acceptable.

The fashion shows – in New York, London, Milan and finally Paris – were a nightmare. When I got to my room at the Hotel Montalembert in Paris, the very place Fabrice deposited Linda in *The Pursuit of Love*, for the first time, I thought I had stumbled into a funeral director's instead: my room was stuffed with the heady scent of blooms. There was no space left even for me, a recovering anorexic. In Milan, I received a Prada bowling bag, a Tod's evening bag . . . in all I counted 15 bags, all bigger than the bags received by the more junior members of my team. I received a Louis Vuitton traveller worth £1,700, with an LJ on the handle, embossed in gold. At first, I thought they had made a spelling mistake with their logo, until I realised the LJ meant me. I must have arrived, surely? The gifts make you feel all warm and fuzzy inside when you come to write your catwalk show review. Ever wondered why all the glossy editors applauded when animal rights protestors were dragged by their hair from the Burberry catwalk by bouncers? They each had shiny Burberry totes at their toes, delivered that morning to their hotels. I was invited to Alberta Ferretti's palazzo and told to choose an outfit. I chose a pair of buttery suede Pocahontas trousers, which were duly dispatched in tissue paper to my room, with another pair snuggled alongside, in case the first developed a smudge. Even at the time, I veered between feeling flattered and important, to feeling debased, bought and ghastly. At a lunch hosted by Tamara Mellon for Jimmy Choo in LA, $50 vouchers for her shoes were left on every plate. The young lingerie designer sitting next to me said, 'Do you want mine? I only ever wear Louboutins.'

Fashion gifting, where a celebrity or fashion journalist is given a product in exchange for wearing it out and about, is nothing new, of course. Bon Jovi at the height of their fame went to the Dolce & Gabbana factory in Italy and each band member was given £25,000 worth of clothes. Actually, the Italian duo seem to be among the most generous of all: when Victoria Beckham lost her luggage at Heathrow, her stylist called Dolce & Gabbana and asked if they could 'help'. Of course they did, rushing a complete wardrobe of new clothes to her home, completely free of charge.

As an editor-in-chief, I always had to sit in the front row at a show. If I had not been assigned a front row seat, my team and I (they all sat behind me) would have to flounce out, with as much disruption and treading on gel-French-pedicured toes as possible. I had a town car and chauffeur to ferry me around. At first it was fabulous: the parties thrown by Donatella Versace at her palazzo in Milan, where you would stand in line for the buffet behind the likes of Carmen Kass and Karolína Kurková (you were never terribly worried they'd leave those further back in the queue with nothing to eat). I remember being backstage after that Versace show, hearing Angela Lindvall, a gorgeous model who had at that time a little bit of a skin problem, being told she'd have to lose weight, as her hips were so wide, they feared she never fit on the catwalk. There wasn't an inch of fat on her. At the show earlier in the evening, Trudie Styler and husband Sting had sat front row, and I'd noticed she'd hung on to his arm, like a child on the end of the string of a helium balloon, in case he bobbed towards the supermodels. Later there was the weekend trip to a spa in Capri, courtesy of Tod's, with a yacht tethered in the harbour, waiting to cruise you around the island. My path to a hilltop restaurant was lit with teeny

Diptyque candles. One of my companions, from a rival glossy, remarked, screwing up her nose, 'I think the candles really fight with the scent of the lemon trees.'

The brands' PRs would practically lick my shoes every time I turned up at a show or an event. A prophetic freebie was when I was invited to Babington House in Somerset on a jaunt held by the owners of Clarins. I was bowled over by the beauty of the house. I had the room in the skylights, with its own wooden terrace and outdoor hot tub, its flat screen TV and herb garden. The only thing missing was someone to share it with. I vowed to come back one day and that then my life would always be like this, all waffle cotton pillows and massages and heated pools. (When I did return with my future husband, he moaned that it was too windy to go on the wooden terrace, preferring to stay inside watching the football. You can take a boyfriend to Babington House, but you sure as hell can't make him take an oily bath against his will.)

Some of the events and shows were glorious – the Alexander McQueen show in September 1999, entitled Eye, at Chelsea Docks in New York, where the models seemed to walk splashily on water. Or his show in London, on 26 September 2000, entitled VOSS, where the catwalk was encased in an enormous glass box, which meant we had to stare uncomfortably at our own reflections as we sat in the front row, waiting. The models, unable to see out of the box, were depicted as patients in an insane asylum, wearing headbands and pearl cocktail dresses. At the end, another cube revealed an obese nude woman, face in a mask, breathing through a tube, surrounded by moths. 'Sublime' was American *Vogue*'s verdict.

Of course, all this generosity came with an enormous price tag. Used as I was to the attitude of a newspaper when it came to featuring a brand (the brand is lucky to get the exposure and we, the journalists, are unimpeachable in pursuit of the truth), I soon found out that glossy magazines are merely elaborate press releases. There was never any thought to what the reader might find interesting, only what will sell more advertising and keep the gifts coming. On my first Christmas as editor, I received the following:

Ivory silk Nicole Farhi bed linen

A wicker sun bed from Gucci (useful!)

Twenty handbags from various designers, including

Chanel and Prada

The list went on and on and on.

I also made mistakes with my cover choices. After the heady sales of my Victoria Beckham cover in October 1999 (shot by Demarchelier, this issue sold nearly 500,000) and the *Friends* cover, I gave Heidi Klum the honour. I was intrigued, looking at the contact sheet of cover tries (these were the days before digital cameras when we had to budget for the amount of film a photographer would use), that she had crow's feet. We airbrushed them away. She still sold very badly.

At the same time, we shot Sade, then a 40-year-old star, for the cover. I was in Milan when the page proofs were couriered to my hotel room (emailing was still difficult and time-consuming – I had to take phone socket plugs for every different country with me, to hook up my heavy laptop, and dial up local, foreign telephone exchanges to make a connection). She looked her age, but still beautiful. My publisher vetoed putting her on the cover as 'She looks like an old crone.'

The worst aspect of *Marie Claire*, though, was the management. Half the magazine was owned by the French, a private family company, the Prouvosts, and so several times a year I had to catch the Eurostar and attend board meetings. The French matriarch, Evelyne, daughter of the magazine's founder, Jean Prouvost, was fearsome. Over lunch, she couldn't understand I was vegetarian and would merely get the waiter to proffer the vegetables swimming with meat gravy. (I have just typed 'Evelyne Prouvost dead' into Google, in a vain hope. I'll try again tomorrow. Whoever said I'm not an optimist?) I once told her that my fashion director, whom I think she liked and admired and who had worked for the magazine for many years, having first trained at *Vogue*, was off on her second maternity leave and I was currently deciding who on earth to hire temporarily in her stead. As she fingered the ropes of Coco Chanel pearls around her emaciated neck, I couldn't help wonder whether she was considering firing her.

The elderly French women, in their fearsome uniforms of Chanel cardigan suits, also did not understand the British market. When I showed them the issue with Victoria Beckham on the cover, then the hottest star in the UK, they exclaimed, 'Oo eez thees? Victoria Beckham, ooo eeez she?'

I never fought for what I knew was right. When I, at last, secured Natalie Portman for a cover, dressed by Stella McCartney, the cover photo immediately stood out: a breathtakingly beautiful close-up shot of her face. 'Wow!' I said to Peter Winterbottom, the art director. 'This is the best cover we've done so far. Can you mock it up using the colour version?'

'Um. There is no colour version. The photographer only shot her in black and white.'

Oh, dear, but no matter! I had the brilliant idea, as the shot was for the Christmas issue, of adding gold to the mast head, so it stood out and shimmered in relief. The publisher vetoed the cost. At the board meeting, hauled over the coals for the weaker, full-length shot of Portman, I didn't stick up for myself and show the cover I hadn't been allowed to print because of the cost.

We were bastardising all the images as well. At our repro house one day, I saw a young man who worked on my magazine taking away the nose from a cover shot for *Vogue* and replacing it with another one. 'You can really do that?' I asked him. 'We do it all the time.'

After a great deal of chasing, Kerry and I had managed to secure Renée Zellweger for our April 2001 cover, in advance of the first Bridget Jones film. The wording on the spine of my magazine had been 'The only glossy with brains'; for this issue, I changed it to, 'The only glossy with Bridget'. (In a fit of pique, after I was sacked, I changed it to 'The only glossy with Brians'.)

The shoot was done in LA with Matthew Rolston. I did the interview in the lobby of the Mondrian hotel, mainly because I was sick and tired of writers telling me they wouldn't fly to LA unless it was business class, or were too busy picking up their child from school. I remember we ordered flat organic rain water. I finally knew I'd arrived.

But the shoot was a disaster. Rather than Bridget turning up, all creamy cleavage and chipmunk face, in her place was someone very slight indeed. All the strapless ball gowns by Versace and Armani (what can I say? I caved) merely exposed her slim frame. Dresses bagged and sagged. But we had no choice, we had to carry on with the shoot.

Back in London, when I finally saw the developed film, I was aghast. Zellweger was barely smiling in any of the photos. She looked so far from resembling the puppyish Bridget Jones, drastic measures were needed, and so we had to air-brush her to make her look bigger.

All the celebrities we featured gave me gip. Photographing Victoria Beckham in Paris, Demarchelier had taken a lovely black-and-white picture of her holding her new baby, her first, Brooklyn. The heading above the interview was: 'When Posh Came to Shove'. Her PR, Caroline McAteer, had told me before the shoot that any pictures of the baby were strictly out of bounds. When I saw this shot, I got Patrick to print it as a one-off, had it framed (okay, I got Kerry to take it to be framed) and couriered it to Victoria's London house with a note, saying, 'I hope you enjoy owning the photo, the negative of which has been destroyed.' She didn't even say thank you. Another star borrowed a Ferretti gown for a red carpet awards show and returned it covered in paint.

I'd been becoming more and more disillusioned with the whole business of fashion and magazines, two altars I had worshipped at my entire life. I spent most of my time in meetings with management, endlessly debating the merits of this free gift on the cover over that. A free notebook took up more time than securing the star for the cover and shooting all the fashion: the 101 ideas and the Runway to Roadway pages. In the end, it was a Dior show in Paris that opened my eyes, that tipped me out of my fearful lethargy. A new super-model had walked the catwalk. She was Gisele Bündchen, and she was so very different from all the other girls: bronzed, with round, high breasts, where all the other models had none. I went backstage after the show (a strange tradition – a scrum where you battle backstage to air kiss the designer and drink Champagne, while all around you 16-year-old girls stand naked) and went up to Gisele to introduce myself (she had been on our cover, her first, in 1998). I hugged her. I couldn't believe what I was feeling: she was a husk, like a baby sparrow. It proved to be a turning point. She wasn't curvaceous at all. Like everything else in the world of fashion, she was an illusion.

Then an accident happened. For the June 2000 cover, I had shot Pamela Anderson, naked, covering her breasts with her arms. Under pressure for our sales figure not to drop, we had secured a shoot with Sophie Dahl, who had not long trod the Galliano catwalk – the one voluptuous model we'd seen all decade. I called the art director, Peter, into my office, a flea-bitten warehouse loft, just over the road from the King's Reach brown tower.

'I want you to shoot Sophie Dahl in exactly the same pose as Pamela Anderson. The same photographer, make-up artist, background, the works.'

'Okay. But will she go naked?'

'We will ask.'

Sophie's agent agreed to the pose, but said she wanted the model to wear a nude bra, which could be airbrushed away later.

The shoot was duly done and I had two identical covers in front of me. Lucinda, the managing editor, investigated the cost of publishing two covers: it would only be about £400. I then wrote the cover lines: Which cover star do you prefer? The impossibly perfect, or the realistically curvy?

Both covers came out, and the reaction was huge. I wrote a piece in the *Daily Mail*, my first for that paper – I talked about my battle with anorexia and about the shock I had felt when I had hugged Gisele, then the biggest model in the business, celebrated for her curvy figure, and realised how small she actually was: every single news-paper featured our experiment and ran stories by writers about anorexia, about the model industry, and what should be done about it.

I was rung by the government's then Minister for Women, Tessa Jowell, to ask whether I would help put together a 'body summit', where all the editors, photographers, designers and model agents would be called to a conference at Westminster. Of course I said yes.

That day, sat on the minister's right-hand side, having dodged TV cameras outside, the debate began. A group of teenage girls turned up and begged everyone in the room to 'stop doing this to us'. Lisa Armstrong of *Vogue* and *The Times* (now fashion editor of the *Daily Telegraph*), stood up to say that models in the Sixties had also been thin. What she failed to point out was that the vogue for young women to look like Twiggy had lasted barely three years: in those days, as designer Barbara Hulanicki later told me, 'Young women expected to grow up, get married in their early twenties, and look like their mothers. There was no desire to stay permanently child-like.' Gisele's agent stood up and said I had no right to call his client 'a bag of bones'. Fiona McIntosh, then editor of *ELLE*, stood up to say she had been bullied at school for being thin. (She later put Calista Flockhart on her cover with the tag line, 'I'm thin, so what?')

The minister, seeing it wasn't going well, slipped me a note. On it, it read that I should stand up and suggest we start a committee of editors, agents, designers and photographers who would monitor standards for the whole industry. I told Jeremy Langmead, still editor of Style (his deputy, Robert, had once taken a job on a magazine called *Dolly* in Australia just so, when the phone rang, he could pick it up and say, 'Hello, *Dolly*!'), I'd done this purely because I'd been prompted. 'I thought it was out of character,' he said.

Back in the office the next day, Kerry brought a fax into my office. Her face was grim. All the other editors, agency bosses and designers had signed a letter, saying they would have nothing to do with any monitoring of their own industry. My fight was over. I could no longer get through to anyone in Tessa Jowell's office: they simply blanked me.

More bile was yet to come. In Paris for couture, a fax landed on my bed. It was a copy of an interview with Sophie Dahl, published in the *Daily Mirror*, in which she stated that she had had her bra straps airbrushed on the cover without her knowledge or consent, and she had never agreed to be naked, or to be part of our anti-skinny models campaign (which is basically true, but only the final part, since she lost most of her body fat over the next year or so). She did know her ugly, nude bra straps were going to be excised, though, as there had been much discussion on the shoot. Also, who would publish a photo clearly showing ghastly underwear? But, long after I had left *Marie Claire*, I was still being summoned to the office by the legal team to discuss the case, which, in the end, IPC settled for £10,000 out of court.

But something had also happened on the personal front. I had started a column in *The Sunday Times* Style, beginning on Millennium Eve, when a man, who soon became referred to only as 'the Osama Bin Laden lookalike', stood me up. Called 'Single File', the column was all about being 'the real Bridget Jones'. Except, miracle of miracles, I was not single for long.

At *Marie Claire* I hired an entirely unsuitable music critic because I fancied him, but when I asked him to go with me to Jamaica, to stay in Ian Fleming's house, courtesy of Aveda, he demurred. (Ever wondered why there are so many spa features in the back of your glossies? It means the editor wants a holiday and a detox but can't afford to pay her own way as she has already spent too much on her nanny.) So I asked a young Indian reporter from the BBC, Nirpal Dhaliwal. He had originally come into my office in April 2000 to ask me about an upcoming award for challenging racism in the media (I had put a black woman on the cover), but he was really only interested in checking out the women who worked on the magazine. He took me to see *Being John Malkovich* and actually HELD MY HAND. He said yes to the free holiday and duly turned up at the door of my Hackney house (I had been able to afford it as it was on the corner of a street with the worst figures for knife crime in Europe) with his rucksack and a keen expression. He endeared himself to me when, at the airport, he had said, returning from a foray to Boots, 'I've bought four hundred condoms. D'you think that will be enough?'

But as I was closing my suitcase to leave my house on that Saturday morning, for my first holiday in years, and my first EVER with a man, the phone rang. It was the news desk of *The Sunday Times*. 'Is it true that Tessa Jowell passed you a note suggesting a committee, it was not your idea at all? Why are you in the pocket of the Labour government?'

Jeremy had told his newspaper! I set off on my holiday in a state of extreme stress and fear; yet another default setting off the scale of normality, of sanity, or liveability.

Of course I was sacked not long after this debacle. A new MD had taken over and he wanted his friend, Marie O'Riordan, who had once edited *ELLE* and was currently magazine-less, to take my place. Rita Lewis asked me to lunch and picked me up in her town car from my office. She was weird as we drove over Waterloo Bridge towards the restaurant Axis, beneath the One Aldwych hotel.

'They want you to step down,' she told me, tears in her eyes.

What you brood on will hatch. 'Really? Why?'

But it was obvious why. We returned to the Tower, where the big boss offered me six months' money, and said I could leave that afternoon. 'I would rather finish the current issue,' I said. 'It will only take a few days.'

I returned to my office. Kerry could see by my face something was up, and she came in and closed the door and the blinds. Peter came in, too, and Michelle, my level-headed deputy, repository of much suede Alberta Ferretti. I left not long after. Unlike the funeral parlour that greeted me upon my appointment, tellingly not a single daffodil arrived on my desk in commiseration or solidarity.

Stupidly, I expected everyone I had hired – the Kate Thorntons, the Bridget Freers – to leave in solidarity, but of course they didn't. They probably had mortgages to pay; it hurt me nonetheless.

On the day I was sacked, I got home to the house in Hackney and told Nirpal, who had moved in with me, along with his vast collection of trainers, that 'They want me to step down.' I burst into tears. He carried on standing there, grazing from the fridge, and said, 'You always hated that job anyway.'

I quickly spent my redundancy money on my new boyfriend. I took him on holiday to the Villa San Michele, overlooking Florence, where he splashed me in the infinity pool. The cost of the room was insane but, like the rest of my life, it was not perfect: it was in the new wing, not the old part of the hotel. Not for the first or last time in my life, I had room envy. It was while I was sat eating orange-yolked eggs for breakfast on my own that I got a phone call from an editor at the *Observer*. '*Nova* magazine has just folded,' he said. 'Can you write a piece for us?'

Jeremy, on my recommendation, had not long been appointed editor of this magazine, relaunched by my boss at IPC, Rita Lewis, and so I wrote a badly misjudged piece for the *Observer* on why it had failed. Like *Marie Claire*, it always had to play second fiddle to *Vogue*. I hadn't meant to criticise Jeremy, but he took offence.

I started life as a freelance, writing from home. I had, by this time, six mouths to feed, having acquired two more tabbies: Susie and Sweetie. It was September 2001. I was at my desk when the Twin Towers went down and my future husband spent all day on the phone to his friends, exclaiming in glee that now the world would change for the better. I knew it wouldn't. I was jealous of all the fashion editors in New York for this momentous occasion. I suddenly wished I'd been there, too.

In that first year of freelance work I earned £27,000, almost back to my *Mirabella* days of over a decade before. It was hard, humiliating. I missed the camaraderie of the office – a boyfriend who was a monosyllabic nightmare and who mainly stayed upstairs looking at porn (which, the internet then being dial up, was expensive), was not great company. But, having to pay for both of us, I took any job that came my way. For one feature, I was sent out with a fake pair of breasts, the very ones worn by Renée Zellweger in the *Bridget Jones* movie to see how different life was with boobs. I was sent to interview David Cassidy in Las Vegas. His son came across me rummaging in his dad's wheelie bin for a memento before the interview, and ushered me nervously inside to meet a man who was nothing like my childhood idol: he had no sense of humour and was only interested in watching horse racing on a large screen TV. I asked him why he had lost the feather cut and he became even more tetchy.

I soon started to work for the *Evening Standard* again, first as a freelance writer, then as editor of Life and Style, when my tweedy protégé Jeremy Langmead, who had moved from *Nova* to *ES*, left to edit *Wallpaper** magazine. I appointed Kerry Smith as my deputy: anyone who could survive three years as my PA on *Marie Claire* deserved not just a job but a medal. I would arrive at the office, Edina-Monsoon-fashion, barking into my mobile phone that I was entering the build-ing. Kerry's main job on the paper was to 'chase' celebrities. She had spreadsheets on her computer, which would alert her when it was time to chase someone again, or would tell her when she last did so, given I would ask her, 'Have you chased Ian McEwan/husband of dead Liz Tilberis/Geri Halliwell recently?' about six times a day.

There was a ghoulishness about working on the tabloid. We were always chasing not just celebrities, but real people who had fallen on bad times. We said that if Emine Saner, a beautiful young writer with Gisele Bündchen hair and a sympathetic expression, turned up on your doorstep wielding flowers, tragedy must have befallen someone in your immediate family. We didn't use the names of our subjects as we discussed chasing them, just their defining tragedy; thus we were in hot pursuit of 'Coma Boy', 'Drowned Honeymoon Bride' and 'Breast Cancer Lady'. The worst moment for journalistic integrity came on the morning of 7/7, when reports started to come in about a bomb on the Underground and on a bus. The buzz of anticipation settled over the newsroom. We immediately swung into action, sending reporters to the danger zone. I remember dispatching Emine to the casualty department of the East London Hospital with the instruction to 'interview anyone in bandages' ringing in her shell-like ears. On her leaving card, a mocked-up *Evening Standard* front page, she eventually earned the headline 'I don't want to do this stupid story!' and the by-line 'Poor me!' I once made her go to New York to interview Matthew Broderick, recalcitrant, publicity-shy husband of Sarah Jessica Parker. 'I got three minutes with him and he wouldn't mention Carrie Bradshaw once,' she moaned to me. On the way to JFK, her taxi was in an accident, meaning she got whiplash. I mounted a campaign to have her photographed in her neck brace, so it could be worn as a more empathetic by-line photo above the more serious stories. The editor refused my request. From 8/7 on, our spreadsheet included the names of everyone who was injured in the blast, and the families of the dead, and we would ring them, without fail, on every anniversary, dredging up the past with unrelenting and probing frequency.

All stories had to have a personal, therefore slightly female, angle. By now writing the interviews, as every other female writer with a pulse had disappeared on maternity leave, I managed to secure a 'chat' (this was what interviews were called in features conference, belying the Herculean effort on Kerry's part in securing them, while photographs were called 'snaps') with Imran Khan, former husband of Jemima Goldsmith. God knows how. (Actually, in hindsight, I probably offered him a weekly column, a common ruse, quickly snapped away, like a tablecloth conjuring trick, the moment the 'chat' was in the bag. I did the same to Alexandra Tolstoy, to get the story of her marriage to a mounted Cossack of inferior funds. To this day, she still phones Emine asking when exactly her column is going to start.) There had just been an earthquake in Pakistan; in the trade, this is not a tragedy, it is a 'peg'. I flew to Islamabad, a shalwar kameez in my luggage I'd been too busy to buy myself, so had secured the services of a lifestyle management coach, who also went and queued for my visa. When I arrived at the airport, I was aghast that men in nighties were trying to get a steer of my Louis Vuitton case and that the hotel didn't serve alcohol. The meeting with Imran Khan was somewhat shady, given I had only a go-between. One morning, I was told to meet him at Khan's political office, a decidedly run-down, badly carpeted place in the middle of town.

The photographer, a local man, and I then had to get a taxi and follow the go-between in his battered old car. We travelled for hours along unmade roads I thought had been shattered by the earthquake but apparently were always like this. Eventually, we arrived at Imran Khan's palace, a beautiful house on a hill, with parched landscaped gardens. The man himself walked across the lawn, dressed in khaki shorts, shirt open at his neck, his two blond sons in tow. (Small family members of publicity-shy celebrities are known in the trade as 'bingo'.) We sat on his terrace and I fired questions about the earthquake at him. He and his sons had already been down to the city of tents to speak to those stricken by the disaster and hand out blankets and supplies. He was very critical of the president, Musharraf, whom he accused of siphoning off the relief funds for his own, private use. At the end of the afternoon, I asked him about his children and the breakdown of his marriage. The next day, I went to the earthquake zone by taxi, aghast no one from the city was just driving there, cars filled with blankets and food. Children were dying of infection from simple fractures. Some even had gangrene. I visited the hospital in the city, where beds had two or three children upon them, then returned to the hotel pool to sip virgin cocktails and eat pineapple. When I got back to

London, I filed my copy. The editor swept up to my desk (an action that always instilled fear and much closing of websites among all on my section), and said, 'It's fantastic, so much about Jemima and the sons. And, there I was, thinking it would all be stuff about the earthquake!'

It would not be the first time I had sold my soul, and the souls of the people I wrote about.

The editor was the fearsome Veronica Wadley, who had moved to the *Standard* from the *Daily Mail* to take over from Max Hastings. I wanted not to be scared of her, so christened her Mummy, which soon caught on, as the whole of the newsroom started calling her this. We had a features conference every morning at 10am, after the first edition had gone to bed. (I never did get the hang of all the West End Finals and City editions, but merely hoped no one would die in the middle of the afternoon, which meant we would all have to stay late: Dr David Kelly was found at EXACTLY the right time to prevent me getting home in time for *EastEnders*.)

The pressure to fill the paper with stories not just every day, but two or three times a day, given all the different editions, was immense. The difference between a tabloid and a broadsheet can be summed up thus: we need even the most banal of arts interviews to have an edge, a hidden tragedy, a revelation. Unlike a broadsheet, we were expressly not allowed to be sycophantic and boring. And if the interviewee would not play ball, we would dredge up something from the distant past. Take the novelist Ian McEwan: I had managed, thanks to Kerry and her spreadsheet, to secure the first interview with the award-winning writer to coincide with his new novel *Saturday*. Lucy Cavendish was assigned the piece. She is a wonderful writer with a great sense of humour and a cast-iron refusal to ever knowingly schedule an interview, even with Hillary Clinton, that conflicts with the School Run. Her determination to juggle her work and home life is always something I have admired. But in the article, Lucy failed to dig up, again, like Richard III's remains, the full details of how he had left his wife. The editor felt this was a huge omission, even though said divorce had been well chronicled in the past. We then not only broke the embargo, meaning the publisher's schedule for publication was in tatters (tabloids always have to be first), we also inserted lots of stuff about the break-up and published a headline and a photograph of the author and his ex-wife that reflected this ancient event. The author, in fact every author represented by the same publishing house, never spoke to the *Standard* again.

Chapter eleven

'COME ON, OLD LADY! MIND THAT HIP!'

I had lunch with Katharine Viner, then editor of *Guardian* Weekend, and now the *Guardian*'s deputy editor. We'd briefly been colleagues on *The Sunday Times Magazine* before she'd been whisked off to stardom. She offered me a column, called 'The Wedding Planner'. It would come out every Saturday with an illustration, and would chronicle my journey to the altar.

There were just two problems.

The first, that my much-younger (he was 26, I told him I was 37) boyfriend had yet to propose. The second, that it only paid £100 a week. But I was desperate. My live-in (I just typed 'love in' by mistake, but it really wasn't like that) boyfriend had proved vastly expensive. An old Golf VW. Food. Dinners at the Organic Pub. You name it, I bought it. So I took the job. I wrote the column.

Nirpal and I got married in October 2003, at Babington House. He later denied ever asking me to marry him, protesting he had been pushed into marriage, learning about it for the first time when he saw I had booked the country house spa in Somerset. But he did ask me, sort of. I have the email here: 'I want to be tied to you, Chubby.' But at the wedding (at which I wore a cream, cashmere, Helmut Lang tuxedo because I still didn't believe I was really a woman, not a proper one, anyway), by the time I crawled upstairs on my Bottega Veneta Swarovski-crystal-encrusted heels to that room with the hot tub, he was nowhere to be seen. What can I say? It was a pattern. When I woke up the next morning, he was gone; I found him downstairs having breakfast with his black lesbian best friend, Bummi. No one moved over so that I could sit down.

We went on honeymoon to Seville but, as he had only just passed his driving test (I paid for the lessons as well as his car), I had to drive, which I hated, as the road to our freezing cold villa was precipitous, next to a steep drop. He did try, though, at first. He made me coffee in a French press, but having never used one before he pushed it too quickly, so the coffee spilled out and burnt his arm. At the villa, with no telly, a bed like a hammock (we didn't have sex on our honeymoon once; I think I had post-traumatic bride syndrome), me in fear of being phoned by NatWest to say the cheque to Babington House had bounced (I bought our rings, too, and his suit, with its 44-inch waist: he insisted on wearing a black shirt with no tie), we played Eighties Trivial Pursuit on the terrace. I didn't realise he was reading the answers on the back of each card I held up. 'You should really have won,' he said, as he shuffled the pack, 'given the Eighties were your heyday.' Those were the days when his teasing, calling me Old Lady and Chubby (his ironic name for me given my cadaverous silhouette), still made me laugh.

He had left the BBC soon after we met, encouraged by me to write his first novel. But he had too much free time on his hands, while I was always working. I'd get home first from *Marie Claire*, then from the *Evening Standard*, late, and all the lights would be out, so I would have to creep around, like an exhausted burglar. As soon as his book was published, after his super-cool book launch that was filmed by Channel 4 as part of a documentary he was making about racism, we went to India, to stay in a hotel on Lake Udaipur. We were supposed to do yoga and meditate each day but even the sight of me, sat cross-legged, near him, seemed to annoy him, as did a spa treatment we were supposed to endure as a couple, which meant both of us being immersed in a tepid bath with floating petals on the surface. He shoved his meaty thighs on either side of my cowering body, taking up more than his half. He eyed the beautiful Indian women who stood, holding up fluffy towels for us to step into. I left him there, with a digital camera he later complained made him 'too hot', because he wanted to travel for a few months. He was frightened when I was due to go, though, the person who looked after him. I was his mummy, his keeper, or his care in the community social worker, not his wife. But he soon found his feet.

When he came back, three months later, I picked him up from Heathrow. He was sheepish, bashful, full of regret. He said nothing. But I could tell. I read his texts to a number in New York. 'Can't wait to see you.' Over a curry, he mentioned the name of a woman he had met. 'Who is she?' Oh, just someone he had got to know while travelling. When I asked him what she was like and he told me, trying not to smirk, Carrie Fisher's immortal line in *When Harry Met Sally* sprang to mind: 'Oh, you know, thin, pretty, big tits. Your basic nightmare.'

I threw him out. It was the scrolling through the pictures he had taken on the camera that made it real, made me pluck up courage: there she was, blonde, tanned, with friendship bracelets on her slender wrists. There they were on a balcony, laughing, having breakfast. We never laughed on holiday; on any balcony you'd care to name I'd be alone, opposite an empty chair. He even took close-ups of her asleep. Of course, he had been too lazy to delete the evidence. I made such a noise shouting and throwing his things on the pavement that Susie broke the cat flap in her haste to escape. But, of course, two days later he came back. 'Oh, Baby, I love you so much!' He promised me a weekend in New York, which he would pay for. We stayed in the Hudson Hotel. It was freezing. I remember each morning he would disappear, early. I'd hired a private detective to monitor his calls and none had been to her, I was sure of that. But I knew it would happen again.

When we landed at Heathrow, he complained that I had forgotten where I'd parked the car. I should have drawn a map, made a note. My dad would never have made my mum draw a map. I knew it was over.

In 2006, I left the *Standard* for the *Daily Mail*, just one floor up in the building on Kensington High Street. I had, at Nirpal's behest, stopped writing my *YOU* magazine column in the *Mail on Sunday*, and in the March of that year had been sent to Paris to cover the shows for the *Daily Mail* for the very first time. So much had changed since I had last been there. Who was Jessica Stam? Who on earth was Natasha Poly? The models were strangers, all of a sudden. My experience wasn't helped by the fact that the fashion editor of the *Standard* at the time had taken all my show requests off the fax machine, so not a single ticket was waiting for me at my hotel.

I had to beg for tickets and blag my way in, hot tears springing from my newly laser-surgeried eyes. While Paris had always harboured anxiety for me on those dreaded trips to attend board meetings, now it seemed every time I rounded a corner in my difficult shoes, my phone would ring with yet another difficult call. The first was from MP Oona King. I had interviewed her before I left the *Standard* and, although she had asked for what she said to be off record, I had put in the published piece all about her struggles to have a child. Now, on the phone, she was so full of rage she could barely speak. I apologised, but I knew I had betrayed her. I never, ever learned.

I came out of the Hermes show on the Saturday and Nirpal called. He had just been interviewed by *Guardian* Weekend about his novel, and he phoned to tell me he had confessed to the journalist about his affairs. (He had been interviewed by a young woman for the *Independent*, too, who had asked him whether my writing about him made him cross. 'Yes,' he said. The eventual quote in the piece read, 'It makes me cross, cross inside.' He wailed it made him sound like a petulant toddler, which in a way he was.)

Unbeknown to him, I had already written a column about his betrayal, due to be published the very next day in the *Mail on Sunday*. I sort of hoped he just wouldn't see it. That morning, I left my hotel and was on the Eurostar back to London, when my phone rang. It was him. 'You f***ing c***, how could you write about my affair? You said you were stopping the column for good!' I wondered if he was mainly angry I had spoiled the *Guardian*'s scoop.

So, he had just read my column. The newspaper had run a front page headline promoting the column, which read, 'Liz Jones is back! And it's all going horribly wrong for Chubby, Snoopy and the Husband!' He couldn't really have missed it. I felt he deserved it, this betrayal. But, yet again, I had put my work before my private life.

'It's over,' I said.

'No, it's not over,' he said. He still wanted to make it work. I knew it never would. Not because of his affairs, or because of the age difference, but because I am unlovable. Because I am not worth it.

Chapter twelve

'YOU'RE GOING TO LEAVE YOUR HOUSE TO A CAT HOME!'

I was living in a gorgeous Georgian house, with French windows and a balcony in the master bedroom, marble fireplaces, a modernist basement kitchen and black-and-white Timorous Beasties wallpaper in the hallway and on the stairs. I would buy armfuls of white flowers every Friday afternoon and have my 700-thread-count bed linen professionally laundered and wrapped in crisp, brown paper. There was a Nicole Farhi Home club chair in the office. My husband contributed only books to the household décor scheme. I was still living with him, though I did not trust him. But my sister, Sue, was in a far worse state than me.

One evening, when Joe was nine years old, we were sitting

on the grass at Audley End House at a Van Morrison concert, and she told me her partner, Robert, had not slept overnight in their house for two years. 'I thought at first he was staying with his mum, but now I'm not quite so certain. Especially since she's dead.'

I told her this was not acceptable. Maybe I'd watched one too many episodes of *Sex and the City*. Even though they were not married, they had a child and his absence was setting a very weird example. She said she would confront him.

This she did, and it turned out he had been leading a double life. Even though their relationship had always been combustible, to say the least, Sue was devastated when he moved out. I spent many nights on the phone to her from the patio of my lovely house, while my husband was shuffling in his bald Adidas socks inside, making curry and a mess. She said every time Robert came round, they would start fighting. The neighbours had called the police, worried at the noise of their arguments.

I told her I only had one piece of advice. Not to lose her temper. Having grown up with her, I knew this would be her downfall.

Come April 2007, I decided Sue and Joe needed a holiday. I booked two weeks in Africa, on an island called Vamizi (the names scrawled in the guest book before us were Sven-Göran Eriksson and Nancy Dell'Olio, so you get the idea of the sort of place it was: expensive), where Joe could learn to scuba dive, as he would have his tenth birthday while we were away. My husband started to wonder why he wasn't invited, so I said I would allow him to come, as long as he didn't ruin it with his moods and wanderings off. If he did, I warned him, he would have to pay me back the cost of his flight.

The day dawned. We drove to the airport in my BMW (late, of course, due to my husband's ablutions, which meant I had to park as usual in the short stay car park) and met Sue and Joe, who had come by coach, at the check-in. By the time I went to buy coffee, my husband had disappeared, and only reappeared in the queue at the gate to get on the plane. I so badly wanted to make the holiday special for Sue and Joe, at the last minute I paid to upgrade all our seats to Economy Plus.

After a long flight, boarding smaller and smaller planes, a Russian doll of travel, we arrived in Mozambique. Finally, we had to get on a boat, which meant wading into the water. My husband laughed. 'Bet you wish you hadn't worn Prada cut-off chinos now,' he said. On the boat, Sue got seasick and terribly sunburnt. I felt so sorry for her. She'd been so wounded by what Robert had done. This is always my Achilles heel, feeling sorry for someone (there is a new book just out about this very subject: *The Curse of Lovely: how to break free from the demands of others and learn to say no*; a little too late for me, but I recommend it, as I also do *Emotional Vampires: Dealing with People Who Drain You Dry*, *The Outsourced Self* and *Stop Walking on Eggshells: taking your life back when someone you care about has borderline personality disorder*). I forgot the rages, the kicking, the punching, the money I lost leaving behind the house in Saffron Walden, and felt desperately sad for her. It was the same with Nirpal. Early in our relationship, he had begged me not to finish with him, saying he had never had a proper home before. 'Don't dump me, Lizzie.' He would leave me poems on my bed, or secreted in my suitcase to discover when I reached my next hotel. I relented. Even when I'd discovered, on my birthday the year before, my special day, 5 September, that he was back in touch with the other woman (I copied and pasted their correspondence, knowing I would use them later in a column, and emailed her from his account, spitefully telling her that she was 'number five of the six women he's slept with' while in India; he had confessed to this number, mainly I think to make me believe somehow she was not special, different, worth leaving me for), I gave him another chance.

But it was a dreadful holiday. I was so inept at snorkelling, let alone scuba diving (I told the instructor that I didn't like the thought of all that water above my head), that I was tied to the boat with a piece of string. Joe loved it, though. It was my husband, a few days in, who misbehaved. I took a photo of him, sat in a boat, wearing a life jacket, off to scuba dive, and he looked so gloomy and put upon you would have thought he was being taken to a concentration camp. Only three days into the holiday, sat on the beach in this ecological paradise, into which he ground endless cigarette stubs, he told me he had had another affair, with a ghastly work experience woman at the Mumbai Literary Festival.

'Did you use a condom?' I asked him. 'No.' 'So she could be

pregnant?' 'No. I didn't come inside her. She came on to me, by the way. I went round to her hotel room to borrow a book, and she kissed me.'

I'd realised something was wrong when he'd got back from that literary festival. He kept opening the huge steel fridge door and staring into it, then shutting it. He was moody.

'I knew it!' I said, almost glad our marriage was going to be over, having spent years, Sisyphus fashion, pushing him up a hill towards success and lovely things from the Conran Shop. 'What was her name?'

'Mumble mumble.' It was by now getting dark and, being partially deaf, I could no longer lip-read.

'Spell her name!' I said, and he did.

'N-A-D-I-M-A.'

How stupid he was, as this meant I could later Google her and accuse her of sleeping with my husband, and look up her photo, and be able to describe her in my columns as having a big nose and a low forehead. (In a strange twist of irony, she reported me to the Press Complaints Commission for harassment, yet another example of an overconfident young nightmare who thinks the world owes her a living. I'll bet by the time she is 35 she will be on her second year-long maternity leave.)

I evicted him first from my open-sided log cabin, and then from the island. The night before he left, he sent a waiter to tell me he had taken my passport by mistake, and could he meet me in the morning to swap them over? Who takes a passport from a suitcase relying on only a 50 per cent chance of success?! The next morning, I saw his tiny plane lift above the bay. 'Surprised it could take off!' I yelled. 'Given you are so FAT!' By the time I got back to London, I had filed for divorce.

Come that October, I had sold my Georgian town house and bought a huge (if broken down and unloved and freezing) house in Somerset with land, barns and a lovely garden. I had rescued a racehorse called Lizzie, and had bought the farm in a rush, mainly to give her the perfect home. Only when I had moved in and acquired another pony, Benji, to be her companion, followed by Dream, given to me by a reader who could no longer keep her, did I realise I was doing exactly what I had imagined I would do all those years ago, aged six or seven, sitting on the carpet, moving tiny plastic horses from field to field. Animals were my escape, the only ones I could trust, the only ones I could love and who would love me back.

Nirpal had, in the end, been decent about the divorce. When it was mooted I might have to pay him alimony and give him half the house, I phoned him up and said, 'Just do what you think is morally right.' 'Okay,' he said. 'I don't want a penny.'

But Sue was in dire straits. So, there I was in my big house in Somerset and I had a bright idea. I told her she and Joe could come and live with me. She could have one of my big barns and, with the money from the forced sale of her house, once Robert had taken his half, she could do it up and run a holiday business. She was always complaining about work and the NHS, but loves to cook and have guests. She became very excited about the prospect of running a business, ironing linen, and making everything perfect with Jo Malone products and White Company towels.

Joe was very against the idea, as it would mean moving 250 miles away from his dad and his friends. I told Sue that perhaps she should put the idea on hold, carry on in the NHS, and wait till he was 16 or even 18, and she had retired. She said she didn't want to miss out on his childhood while working, and she would love to live in such a lovely rural place.

So, in February 2008, she and her son moved in. I'd had her and Joe's rooms renovated and a new bathroom put in. I put cherry blossom in her room and a laptop in Joe's bedroom. But, almost immediately, things started to go wrong. She had hired a van that was too small, so had to return to Essex to fetch the rest of her things. She told her friend Jenny that things weren't right. She struggled with anyone who worked for me, such as a gardener or a groom, and she tried to befriend Nic Bebb, an animal behaviourist I'd hired to work each day with my rescued racehorse and who then became my assistant. The build on the barn started. Sue was careful with her money, but as I was paying for all the food and bills, I've no idea why.

In the end, I confided in Nic, as I felt I had to talk to someone about my sister's behaviour. It had been mooted that Nic should rent the barn off Sue but, as we talked, she told me that she couldn't do this. Nic felt this wouldn't work. I told her I didn't blame her, but that I had told Sue I would give her a second chance. 'She has moved all this way, given up her job,' I said. 'I can't just chuck her out. I'm trapped.' I realised I had got myself into another Saffron Walden situation, all over again.

When two women, especially sisters, are at war, it's bad enough. When you add a third, it becomes a nightmare. Lyn was due to stay with us for a few weeks and Sue went to pick her up from Heathrow, as I was working. I'd bought Lyn unguents, a bottle of Alberta Ferretti perfume and a Stella McCartney jacket for when she arrived, as she never had any money, having given up work in Australia to look after her son. She arrived, and the next day, she went off for a drive with Sue, to explore the local moor. When they got back Lyn said, 'Sue is really worried Nic will move into the barn, whereas she'd much rather run it as a holiday let.'

I confronted Sue in the hallway. 'It's your barn; I've given it to you. You can run it as you please when it's finished.'

'Well, the money from selling my house – one hundred and seven thousand pounds – having given Robert his half, is gone.'

'Okay, I can put on hold doing the house up. How much do you think you will need?'

'Fifty grand, maybe more.'

'Okay, but I don't have that amount right now, I will have to save up.' (I'd just had an outdoor ménage put in, for my horse.)

'You shouldn't have spent that money on my outfit for the wedding,' she said. Our niece had just got married and, while I'd leant Sue an Alberta Ferretti dress, I'd bought her Burberry shoes and a clutch, a wrap from Jaeger, and paid for her and Joe to have connecting rooms at a hotel, the Hempel, in west London. 'Oh, I thought you liked the outfit,' I said, shocked.

I paid for Lyn to go up to London on the train to visit our brother, Nick, by then very ill, and to the hairdresser. My instinct was always to pay for stuff, anything to keep everyone happy. I arranged one day to drive Lyn to see Bath, but she made an excuse and said she would rather stay home. I was confused, but I just left it.

Sue became more and more distant. In the end, I phoned my divorce lawyer, Emma, who had always been so quiet, so reasonable, so understanding, through that other domestic episode, my divorce. I told Sue to talk to her too, said the situation between us was getting out of hand and we needed some sort of go-between. But in the end, I had to ask her to leave. I told her I would help her rent a place and eventually buy somewhere. On the day Sue and Joe moved out, a delivery arrived for Joe. Sue signed for the package and Joe excitedly opened it. It was a steel box with a gun locked inside. It was the final insult, the final kick in the teeth, given they both knew how much I love animals and abhorred shooting them for fun. (Actually, the only person to see the funny side in all this was Nirpal. I met him one night at Manna in Primrose Hill for dinner. I was sat, devastated and prim, at the table and he rolled in, performing a fake gun-slinging shoot-out with his fingers.)

So I decided to finish renovating the barn. Maybe then I could sell it and give Sue back the £107,000 she had spent on it. I just didn't have that sort of money. I should have shut the work down, but figured she had told me it only needed another £50,000, and what use to me was a building with no roof? I'd never be able to sell it. Over the next year, with Sue and Joe smouldering in the village not two miles away, I finished the barn. It cost a further £200,000. Every mortgage payment bounced. I put a lot of it on my American Express card, but then that, too, had to be paid. I couldn't pay my tax bill and so HMRC sent in the bailiffs. All I had to sell was my 2003 BMW, which had by now done 200,000 miles driving back and forth to work in London. I couldn't afford to put the heating on. One night, in London for work, I checked into my usual cheap hotel in west London. My card wouldn't work. 'Please,' I said. 'I always stay here.' They told me I needed £50 cash to stay in the room, so I walked to the cashpoint in Westfield Shepherd's Bush to try. All around me were people shopping, lights twinkling, and every card I put in the machine was returned with the message, 'You have zero funds available.' I spent that night on the street: walking, sitting in doorways. I didn't even have the money for a cup of coffee. After 30 years, it had come to this.

Once the barn was finally finished, I put my house on the market. I managed to persuade a bank to lend me the money to buy Sue a house. Why oh why did I do that? (I actually placed my head in my hands as I just typed that last sentence.) I suppose part of it was fear, of retribution of some sort. Part was just trying to play the big 'I am', the all-bountiful, much as I took my husband on an expensive, exotic holiday after he cheated on me. Part, too, was protecting my reputation, given I was, by now, a high-profile writer. I simply didn't want her going to another paper and giving them a sob story that would be believed.

After a year of trying to buy the house she wanted, next to the church in Dulverton, Sue decided she wanted a cottage that had just come on the market by the river: £275,000. She moved in. I was given a year by the bank to sell my house and pay back that loan. I heard, later, that my niece had been to stay in Sue's new house with her baby, that my brothers Philip and Tony had been to Dulverton to see her, but nobody had come to see me. Sometime after she moved out, I received a letter from her friend, Jenny, begging me to help her. When at last I'd managed to buy Sue a house, I called Jenny up. 'I wouldn't normally involve one of her friends but, as you wrote to me accusing me of being the bad person in all this, I want to be sure you know exactly what I have done for Sue,' I told her.

Even after my brother Nick died, in the middle of this debacle, I didn't learn from my mistakes. One of his friends, who stayed with him now and then, called me up. Nick's flat was infested with bugs. Could I help? I paid for it to be fumigated and asked my old London cleaner, H, to spend a few days there, sorting things out. H told me she was shocked at the filth they lived in and that Nick actually slept on a mattress they had found in the road. I wrote a column, probably misjudged but I felt justified, that someone who has been on benefits their whole life could at least keep their home clean. I didn't name the friend; it was more a generalised observation. Nick's friend phoned me up, and shouted at me that Nick had never wanted any contact with his sisters because 'he thought you were all stupid bitches'. Perhaps we were.

Chapter thirteen

QUACK, QUACK. GET
OUT OF TOWN!

21 June 2011: I am at King's Cross station, at the crack of
dawn, about to board a Eurostar train for Paris. I'm at a coffee
shop. I have just sat down at a table, am ferociously guarding
my case, when my mobile rings.

'Is that Liz Jones?'

'It might be. Who is this?'

I never say it's me, because it could be:

a) The man from HMRC
b) The man from HMRC VAT, saying he is at my house
c) My accountant, Amit
d) My bank
e) A stalker or online troll who has got hold of my mobile
   number

f) An irate family member, ex-boyfriend or ex-husband

g) A fashion PR, saying, 'Are you planning any features on how to get that bikini body?' If this were October instead of June, I could expect a call from a fashion PR telling me to 'Think pink for breast cancer awareness' and do I want to customise a T-shirt for a charity auction if they send me the pink poster paint and sequins? In September, like clockwork, fashion PRs ask if I am planning any features on Hallowe'en, Bonfire Night and, ooh, here's a novel idea, Christmas! I've just had one such pop into my in-box with the express purpose of winding me up: 'Find the perfect pampering gift for family and friends with the new Champneys Christmas Collection – a range of luxury collections to treat loved ones.' In January, they ask if I'm planning any features for Valentine's Day. There is one female PR who is probably paid £10,000 a month to send me an email telling me that new research shows drinking coffee is good for you. I'm thinking of reporting her to the police

But no. It's not any of the above. It is ITV.

'Would you be interested in appearing on *I'm A Celebrity, Get Me Out of Here!*?'

My spirits lift. I am giddy with relief. I tell her 'Yes', without having to think about it. I immediately phone Nic, back in Somerset, to tell her we are saved.

*

I arrive in Paris to cover the Galliano trial for the *Daily Mail*. I've booked myself into the Hotel Costes, on rue St Honoré, a stone's throw (or a mere hobble in my new, nude, Swarovksi-crystal-encrusted peep toes by Christian Louboutin) from the Colette store, the sort of eclectic, fiercely edited place that makes me hate not only my shoes, bags, wallet and watch (if I hadn't pawned the Rolex to feed my then husband) but my head, body, limbs and entire life. I've bought things from this store in the past: a DVD of a Cary Grant film that refused to speak in any language other than French; a Chloe ruffled-front blouse for 600 Euros (despite the astronomical price tag, it has really annoying loose threads). Garments in this store, which has a bar in the basement where you can choose from hundreds of different brands of expensive water, are displayed not on rails or folded in neat piles, but on mannequins. Despite the fact that, by now, on the eve of the Galliano trial, I have worked in fashion for 30 years, I'm still a little afraid of these mannequins, even though I know they are not actually real fashion people (despite being called dummies). They make it very hard to read a label, let alone look for a price tag. If you have to look, due to the fact you are surfing very close to your overdraft limit, it involves a weird waltz that becomes a wrestle as you hug the damn mannequin to try to get high enough to look inside the collar.

I'd first stayed at the Hotel Costes while editor of *Marie Claire*, mainly because, on a visit there to have tea with Sadie Frost, I'd discovered it has a pool in the basement. (I'd accompanied Sadie, before our tea of Ladurée macaroons that neither of us touched, to the Chanel show, held in the Hippodrome on the edge of Paris, because we were going to follow her in the magazine, from front row to Oscars red carpet! In the end, though, after many shoots, she rocked up in a vintage dress by no one, scuppering all our plans: typical star behaviour.) I told the executive fashion editor, an ancient woman who knew how to pronounce all the various fashion brand names, such as Loewe 'Loo-Wave-Ay', and Givenchy 'Je-von-shee', and who liked to drain wine glasses as she left a restaurant or fashion launch party, that, from now on, due to the pool, I wanted to stay at Hotel Costes, never mind the expense (800 Euros per night). I don't think I ever swam in the pool once. Actually, I know I didn't. I've never felt comfortable about pools, or hotel lobbies, or bars. I'd look at all the super-confident people, lolling, diving, and wonder at how they seemed so at home, as if they owned the place. Perhaps the cold of Sidmouth beach put me off ever getting into a costume again, but it was more that I always expect to be told off, found out, asked why exactly I'm there, before being told to move back to Essex.

The Costes smells headily of scented candles but, despite these numerous tiny flames, is so badly lit you can fail to recognise your own hand in the lift. I would often start, thinking I was about to be mugged. Which in a way I was, every time I ended up buying a £350 Gucci fitted shirt, one in white, one in black, from the Colette store. I check in, and am shown to my room: it is as dark as a grave. There are no flowers. After my interview with John Galliano for the *Evening Standard* some years before this trial, when he showed me his calendar on the wall (most of the spaces filled in with black pen, indicating the days he was, or was about to be, depressed – even on the blackest days he would jog three miles to the gym, where he would perform hundreds of sit-ups and take part in boxing matches), he had sent me a bunch of roses the size of a hippo with inside out petals: the crimson was on the inside, the pale underbelly on the outside. They seemed strangely cruel, and unnatural, as indeed did he.

But designers are very big on flowers. They also spend a great deal on invitations: stiff, hand-calligraphied billboards encased in scented tissue. My ticket for the Galliano trial is not so fancy when I finally pick it up the next day. Men's Fashion Week is also taking place in the French capital, with Thierry Mugler showing the same day as this show trial, and strangely dressed men with man bags are emerging from town cars, hurrying past in loafers with no socks, ankles exposed.

But despite this proximity, not one solitary fashionista but me is headed towards the Palais de Justice, specifically to Court Number XVII, the very place where Marie Antoinette was sentenced to the guillotine, just the sort of venue John Galliano might have booked for a show for its ornate, macabre quality. I arrive several hours before all the other reporters. They are in jeans, eating sandwiches. I sit, in Dior, looking prim, as an homage: as always, I have gone too far, arrived too early, taken it all much too seriously.

It has been quite a fall from grace for Galliano. Only five

months before, his couture show for Dior had met wide acclaim. 'Opulently swagged tops and gowns bobbed and floated like billowing sails. One utterly gorgeous thing hid roses in clouds of white marabou,' raved American *Vogue*'s online arm, Style.com. 'Dior's New Look was an obvious source point for skirts that flared from corseted waists or dropped pencil-thin to below the knee from rounded hips.' Other words bandied about during this review are 'mesmerising artifice', 'a shimmering depth of degradé' and 'graphite smears, pencil strokes and scribbles, erasure marks, and gouache washes'. Mmmm, lovely. We get the point. You like the frocks. At the end of this show, John took his bow not as a matador, or pirate, as was his wont, but as Al Pacino circa *Dog Day Afternoon*.

Today, in Court XVII, it is now 1pm. A normal man, one with grey hair and an old sweater, who obviously has nothing to do with the world of high fashion, is currently on trial for some small misdemeanour. He becomes more and more nervous, glancing around as the court begins to fill up with members of the world's press. Extra chairs are placed around the edges. Gendarmes, in unbecoming pale blue polo shirts, wielding guns, begin to pace up and down. Laptops are unsheathed, iPads tapped into sentience. How unfortunate this besweatered man is to find himself caught up in the middle of a media storm, the public evisceration, if not actual beheading, of the very best the fashion world has to offer. The man and his solitary lawyer gather their papers and scurry away. 'God, who would want to be famous?' the lawyer says, leaving us. Who indeed.

At 3.40pm, late as always, but not quite enough to be fashionable, John Galliano slips into the courtroom through a heavily panelled side door. The room goes silent. He is accompanied by just one bodyguard. He looks relatively normal, slightly less the Italian-American bank robber: a woman's long blonde hair that, I start to wonder over the course of staring from close quarters for over seven hours, might have been enhanced with extensions (it has certainly been ironed, or 'pressed', as they say in fashion; skiving off in the world of fashion is known as 'an appointment'); an impeccable black jacket (Dior? Now wouldn't that be ironic?); a waistcoat over hairless, bare skin; satin harem pants, like a filled nappy; black brogues; a spotty scarf; and, for a change, no hat. And very little make-up, bar an enhancing of that trademark Clark Gable moustache, and a slick of mascara above those big brown eyes.

You would imagine these proceedings to be very grave indeed, given Galliano, the £4-million-a-year creative director of Dior until he was summarily sacked when arrested back in February, is accused of calling three women anti-Semitic names, but as one such epithet, 'Jewish c***', is read out by one of the three sitting judges, a wave of tittering washes the courtroom, as it does again when lawyers ask for Galliano's bodyguard to be removed for being 'too intimidating'. One accuser, Geraldine Bloch, a museum curator who was sat minding her own business in a café in the Marais district of Paris, was allegedly called a 'dirty Jewish face' and 'Jewish whore'. The designer also stands accused of calling

Bloch's friend, Philippe Virgitti, also here in court today, a 'f***ing Asian bastard'. During proceedings, things seem to be going surprisingly Galliano's way, until the testimony of plaintiff number three. Fatiha Oumeddour is not present in court but, according to her statement, a drunken Mr Galliano had repeatedly called her a 'f***ing ugly Jewish bitch' in a dispute at the same bar the previous October. The English teacher is of Arab origin, but told investigators she 'didn't find the insults funny'.

Two of the women sit in front of me now, and I can see they are just the type Galliano despises: rubbery shoes, short, navy suits, the sort you'd buy on sale in Next, opaque black tights. He had criticised one of the women for the size of her thighs, but she seems perfectly normal-sized to me, simply not a six-foot-tall Amazonian with zero body fat, which is more the type John's used to.

The graduate of Central Saint Martins stands to answer questions. I am surprised, given he has lived and worked in Paris since 1997 – he first moved here to take the helm of couture house Givenchy – that he needs to bend that golden, slightly too-large-for-his-body head to listen to the whisperings of a translator. She soon asks to be excused, saying she cannot understand John's south London accent, which he only seems able to expel from his over-aerobicised chest in a transatlantic whisper. His lawyer takes over her duties. He is asked the first question:

Presiding Judge: Do you remember what happened that night, 24 February?

JG: I don't remember very well. I can't remember very well, I have a memory of a very violent man. I have no recollection [of words used on that night].

PJ: Does he remember who started to be aggressive and utter insult?

JG: I don't remember. I don't remember any insults and how the situation degenerated. I don't remember it lasted 45 minutes.

PJ: Do you remember the driver intervened when the chair was grabbed [Philippe Virgitti, it turns out, was the chair grabber].

JG: I remember that and the arrival of the police.

PJ: How do you explain that this incident lasted for so long?

JG: I don't know.

PJ: How do you explain the fact that you don't remember anything about that incident?

JG: I have a triple addiction. I followed a rehab programme, spent two months in Arizona, I am still being treated and spent two months in Switzerland.

Each time he is asked about the fracas, he says he cannot recall what happened. He blames his behaviour on his dependency on Valium, sleeping tablets and alcohol. He says he is now unemployed, due to Dior's 'zero tolerance' for anti-Semitism. He then goes on to describe his work routine. 'At the time of the financial crash, I have two children. One was

Dior, the other was Galliano. Dior is a big machine and I didn't want to lose Galliano [his company]. At this point in order for that house of Galliano to survive, I met many businessmen and signed many licences. So the collections increased: menswear, women's, children, shoes, boys and girls, perfume projects, jewellery, fine jewellery, beach wear, underwear. The workload increased very fast.'

Galliano is contrite. He says he is sorry for the 'sadness' his behaviour has caused. Another witness, with orange hair and long, gothic skirts, so you just know she is going to be on his side, testifies that, 'I was shocked he lost his job.' Even one of the victims, Geraldine Bloch, says she never meant for the complaint to turn into the media circus it has. She hasn't asked for money, just one Euro, and an apology in the pages of *Vogue* and *Elle*. In the closing speeches, one of the lawyers for the prosecution says he has changed his mind about Galliano, that he seems a 'lost soul'. Galliano's defence lawyer says outside the courtroom, during a recess, that his client 'would not have been aware what he was saying. He would have been hallucinating. He is ill'.

There was a story in the Sunday papers just before the trial, asking why on earth Galliano, clearly troubled, clearly 'ill', was not given help sooner – by his minions, by Bernard Arnault, the owner of LVMH, and therefore the owner of Dior. Why was Galliano allowed to sit in a bar, alone, when his appearance would make him an easy target for the great unwashed? In the video shown in court, the famous segment where Galliano spits that he 'loves Hitler', that the woman in front of him should not really be alive because her relatives should all have been gassed, Galliano wears a stove-pipe hat and astrakhan fur. Galliano always got what he wanted at Dior. If he wanted to send out a different model for every outfit, rather than making each model wear two, three changes of clothes, as is the norm, then he was allowed to do so. His employers had known for a long time that he was out of control, suffering from addiction. In court papers leaked by the prosecution, his chauffeur talks of being 'trained' to call a lawyer whenever John's use of the F word exceeded four every half hour, and things threatened to turn nasty. He was an accident waiting to happen. Which is scandalous, but not unusual. Galliano, after all, had turned a struggling, barely fashionable couture house into a multi-billion-dollar success. It is interesting that he didn't get any help, and sad, but that's just how business is. It covers up the cracks for as long as it can. It is also interesting that he had saved very little of his huge salary; at the time of the trial he was relying on the hospitality of friends and his black American Express card.

But it is Galliano's closing statement in the trial that has made me, the inept outsider, want to write this book. Here it is, verbatim: 'I have all my life fought against prejudice, having been subjected to it myself. I'm passionate and I travel the world not just as a tourist but to understand cultures ... I've lived with Masai tribe ... I travel the world and bring it back in the form of a research book that would become the starting point for the collection.'

What a crock! Those who people the luxury fashion business inhabit a Diptyque-scented bubble where anyone who is not exactly like them is regarded with scorn, as a joke. I don't even think Galliano likes women (for his couture show in autumn/winter 2009 he sent out models with no skirts, obscenely exposing the tops of their stockings in girdles), although he has made it his life's work to dress them. He took the mantra of Christian Dior, who said of women, 'My dream is to save them from nature', about a million miles too far. Unlike Dior himself, who employed house models in their fifties, some with grey hair, Galliano favoured impossibly young, androgynous children.

Anti-Semitism is not new in fashion. Celebrating Nazism is not off limits, because nothing is off limits. Stylist Isabella Blow, whose Diptyque-scented presence wafted through many of my years at *The Sunday Times*, once used a brooch in the shape of a Swastika on a cover shoot. She secreted it in among the fur as a sort of joke. I only noticed it once the cover was published and it was too late to change it. Everything is funny to these people: the stars they dress, the customers, the sky-high prices.

It was Isabella Blow, of course, who spotted the talent of Alexander McQueen and snapped up his graduate collection (John Galliano's 1984 graduate collection, purchased by Joan Burstein of Browns boutique, was called Les Incroyables, which in a touch of unmissable irony was inspired by the French Revolution) and pushed him out into the world, celebrated him. She later committed suicide by drinking weedkiller, having succeeded only in breaking her ankles after leaping from a bridge on the M40 ('Such an ugly road. What was I thinking?'). McQueen, the son of a London cab driver, who once spent £30,000 flying his boyfriend out to join him for his birthday, was also, according to Isabella's widower, Detmar, corrupted by so much power and adulation. 'Money changed him and then drugs changed him,' said Detmar. 'I remember reading of how he had flown his boyfriend somewhere. What did Issy get? Some clothes. I find that quite shocking.'

Fashion, in the end, killed not just McQueen but, in a way, Galliano, because it was all he lived for. I once sat with John Galliano in his atelier on the rue François 1er in Paris, and showed him a video of what happens to a fox skinned for fur to make one of his coats. The video showed the fox, having been electrocuted via its anus, being skinned rapidly and rudely, without ceremony. The camera zoomed in on the creature's face. His eyes, the only part of his body he could move, were swivelling in his head, now a fierce, obscene red. The fox was shocked, clearly thinking, as he looked around, as his fur was stripped from his small body, 'What on earth is happening to me?' At the end of the tape, the fox's long lashes were still blinking, slowly, and John was in tears.

A few months later, I joined the snake of Mercedes nosing out of Paris towards the Palace of Versailles and sat front row in the Orangerie (I loved the fact the gilt chair for Croydon's finest bore the misspelled place name Kate Moose; I often wonder whether any of these people can read), which surely housed the longest catwalk there has ever been. In the distance, you could hear the supermodels before you saw them. Clump, clump, clump, in their impossible laced shoe boots. We strained our necks, not wanting to look too eager, because that would not have been cool. Paraded before my eyes was a scene that closely resembled the first 20 minutes of *Saving Private Ryan*. Entire animals, birds of prey in mid-flight, sat atop each beautiful, empty head. Had John lost his mind? Was he being ironic? Did he have attention deficit disorder, or did he just not like to be shown to be in the wrong? I have no idea.

After the carnage on the catwalk, I joined the other members of the fashion press, the Barneys' buyers, the photographers, the movie stars and the inevitable hangers on, in the gardens, to aerate with our heels lawns that looked as if they had been trimmed with nail scissors. There was a fireworks display, an orchestra playing softly, and teams of chefs stirring what was reputed to be the world's largest paella, and which was probably large enough to be seen from space, in homage to John's Spanish roots. I saw the designer, wandering around alone, Champagne in those long, cool hands. I raised my eyebrows. 'I'm sorry,' is all he said.

I've never inhabited that fashion bubble, where all is scented and well lit and flutes are always brimful of Champagne: I'd merely scratched away on the outside, looking in, denting its sphere every now and then. But I was in thrall to it. I would see Debbie Dickinson, younger sister of

Vogue cover star Janice, in 'Beauty, Health and Slimming' in *Vogue*, eating a watermelon while seated on the deck of some yacht, and I'd then spend my life peeling difficult tropical fruit. I still see a pair of sugar pink Manolo Blahniks on the catwalk (at Emilia Wickstead's Mayfair show, September 2012) and wonder, should I get a cab to his shop in Chelsea and buy a pair? I need a pair. Or a white pair of his patent stilettos? I perform a quick sum in my head, trying to work out the Cost Per Wear, a ridiculous equation dreamed up by those with less money than sense.

It's not just the anorexia that has ruined things, ruled things. And it's not just the expense, the waste, the what on earth for? It's that I hated myself so much, for my entire life, because I never quite measured up, in any way that these people could ever think was meaningful. I never felt good enough to sit front row, start a family, be loved, be naked, take a day off, go in a shop, call down to reception or brave a walkie-talkied bouncer in a fierce black suit. And so I decided to write this book to find out where this hatred started, why I clutched at fashion to save me, and why ultimately it betrayed me, let me down, let me drown. Why it never loved me back. And given it was my mum's biggest fear that when I went out into the world I would be, if not violently murdered, then accidentally mown down by a car, it is interesting and vaguely ironic that the culprit, the person who finally felled me, lived an awful lot closer to home ...

*

Which brings us back to the summer of 2011. I was about to be saved with a huge amount of money, perhaps £200,000, from an offer to appear on *I'm A Celebrity Get Me Out of Here!* The thought kept me going through the rest of that year; I clung on, I occasionally slept all the way through the night. October came round and I got an email from the production company, asking whether I would still be free to fly to Australia over Christmas. Of course I'm still free! What else would I be doing? Then November. Then December. I got a call. Are you still free? Yes! I waited. And waited. Then, as I was driving back to blasted Somerset from London one Friday afternoon, stuck in a two-hour traffic jam somewhere around Chiswick, my agent called. 'You were down to the last three but, in the end, they went with someone else.' I think they plumped (wrong word) for Lorraine Chase, my Eighties doppelgänger.

It was the final straw. I beat my head against the steering wheel, literally. I didn't know how I could go on. I looked at the fuel gauge and calculated, if I cruised on vapours for the last 40 miles, I might be able to make it home without having to buy fuel, for which I had no money.

A couple of weeks later, in the last week before Christmas 2011, I got another phone call. It was from the producer of *Celebrity Big Brother.* Would I like to go inside the house? We think you'd be fabulous. Yes, oh God, yes. My agent was involved and a fee of £300,000 agreed. On the Friday before Christmas, on the day of my *Daily Mail* office party, I was biked the contract. I signed it. I blew on the ink to make it dry, like making a wish. That evening, I dressed up in my black McQueen trouser suit and 10-year-old Prada heels, and met my agent at the Groucho Club, a place I never frequent. I never have time.

I sat down in the bar. For the first time in nearly five years, I felt as if a huge weight had been lifted from my shoulders. As I stood on the kerb to catch a taxi to my office party, I saw all the party-goers streaming through the streets, laughing. I no longer felt separate. I felt like a normal person. Liberated. Without a huge mountain of debt. Almost happy. After almost five years of a waking nightmare, I was at the end of it. I called Nic, who as well as being my assistant is also a friend, and had stood by me every step of the way during my five-year horror film, told her I'd signed the contract and transferred £1,000 to her account, a festive bonus. She was in tears, for me and for her.

When I drove back to Somerset on the Saturday and pulled up outside my gate, for the first time I did not have chest pains, stomach lurching, as I passed the post box, where I knew bills were lurking. It had all been worth it, after all. The 2am shifts at *The Sunday Times*, surviving only on corn-flakes. The long flights across the Atlantic in economy. The 4am wake-up calls to go and work at the *Evening Standard*. The cartoon published in the *Guardian* after *Marie Claire* sacked me, depicting me skating on thin ice. The pressure, the stress, the deadlines, the loneliness, all of it. The overexposure of my marriage and my body. The overexposure of my husband's body, too. (I always defended myself and my writing of him with the excuse that it was all supposed to be funny, viz.: 'Yes, I wrote that you have feet like flippers, but I also added a compliment, that you must be able to swim well.') I'd even had a face lift, documented in print, showing my before and after face devoid of make-up; a game of two halves. This photo montage has somehow ended up on my laptop and, every time I search for a document containing 'Liz', it pops up, revealing itself to me, when we all know I would rather slide along a wall than look at an image of my own face.

It seemed there was nothing I wouldn't do, no one I wouldn't betray, to fulfil the demands of a story. No one now spoke to me. My ex-husband, tired of being dragged up by me in print, ceased all contact, even when my 24-year-old cat, Squeaky, who had been more than a daughter to me, died. She had had fluid on her tummy and lungs, probably from a long-standing tumour. She was really only ill for two weeks, in the end, unable to eat, or climb out of the cat litter tray. She began to smell. I didn't want to let her go. She didn't want to leave me. One day, she lay on the bed on her side, mouth open, panting. The vet arrived to put her to sleep and I held her, my tears making her fur slick and wet. My friends have all disappeared, one by one. I'm not in touch with the gang from those early days in London. I went to Karen's wedding, though, and I know she has a daughter. I follow Chris and Bob's careers – TV series, minor films – but doubt they follow mine. I'm sad when I read Bob has divorced, or a series of vintage drama *The Royal* has been cancelled. They all had so much promise. I lost touch with India Knight after I left

Marie Claire and yet one of my readers sent me a cutting from the *Evening Standard*, with a headline proclaiming the 'Queens of Fleet Street' are at war. Are we? I wondered. It turned out she had called me a 'rancid c***' who 'masturbates her cats' on Twitter. She also referred to me as Nana, due to my age, and said, 'Jeremy used to laugh at her. Now he loathes her.' I was hurt. It was just one more entry in my catalogue of betrayal.

But the truth is, I have had the career I've had because I needed the money.

That Christmas 2011, I thought I was saved, I thought the nightmare was over.

But then the £300,000 TV contract fell apart. My editor at the *Mail on Sunday* told me I shouldn't do it. That it would ruin my career. 'But I need the money. I've had to buy my sister a house. I was protecting my reputation, even though I did nothing wrong.'

And so I was tipped back into the mess. Looking back, I can see how stupid I was: I never protected myself. I've talked about what happened with a couple of people and they say that the same thing happened to them: the moment they were seen as successful, family members tried to take it all away from them. It is especially common when a woman is seen to have success – other people assume you don't deserve it, not if you don't have children.

I've eventually been able to sell my house, at a huge loss. After paying off my mortgage and some of the loan on Sue's cottage, I'm left with nothing. I am having to rent some-where for me and the cats and dogs, and the horses are going into livery. I no longer even have a car, as I ruined the engine of my BMW by driving through a flood at the end of my road. Not for the first time have I thought, why have I no skills, no common sense? Why did no one, not my dad, not my teachers at BCHS, not Charles the Law Lecturer, not Kerry, not my ex-husband, not Nic, tell me that if I drive through water it will ruin a car's engine? That if I give people stuff, they will throw it back in my face, and want more and more and more?

I was talking to a friend the other day, over dinner, after yet another god-awful, boring fashion launch, where everyone stands around on tall shoes, hating each other, trying to guess each other's salary, noticing the freebies on their feet and hanging from their shoulders, and she said that other women, like my sister, are jealous of me. 'But why would they be jeal-ous?' I asked her. 'I work really hard. I rarely get a weekend or an evening off. I have no friends, no family, no children.'

'But they perceive you to be very lucky. You stand there, slim and young-looking, in your designer clothes, you have this amazing platform, and they see their lives, and they hate you.' I think she probably meant, 'You have these amazing platforms.'

I remember when I was working with Zoë Heller, or Helen Fielding, or even Georgina Howell, I was never jealous of them. I felt they probably deserved to be where they were, and I felt it was my job as an editor to make them better, help them, support them. When I met my husband, he wanted to be a writer, and when I read the beginning of his yet-to-be-finished book on that holiday at Goldeneye in Jamaica, I saw he had talent, and I said to him that he should write it. I helped him get an agent, I read every sentence and made what I thought were helpful suggestions. I wore a cream, concertina Chloé top (borrowed!) to his book launch and I was thrilled for his success. But when the *Guardian* ran that interview with him, with the heading, 'Me and Ms Jones', he went insane. 'You old hag!' he screamed at me. 'You imaginary childhood pony old hag!'

I recorded a Radio 4 segment the other day and the interviewer called me the Queen of Confessional Journalism. But I'm not, not really. While it's acceptable to write about your husband cheating on you, and about a messy divorce, and about your own ageing, desiccating body, as I have done, writing about sibling rivalry, about family betrayal, seems to be out of bounds. I haven't written about it before now because it's so shameful. People put it all down to petty squabbles. But in every way I can think of what happened between me and my sister was a million times worse than being divorced. She always had the moral high ground because she had been a nurse, had a son, was a single mum.

My therapist told me the best advice I have ever been given: 'People don't change. If they don't behave as you would like, cut them out of your life.'

I remember one afternoon, for Joe's birthday, Sue invited all the local mums round for tea. I had sat chopping salads and preparing food, while Nic had started up the barbecue, and we were sat with Joe in the garden. Not one of the mums said hello to me or even acknowledged my existence. I was the fashion pariah, they were the unimpeachable mums with the porridge-textured tummies.

I'm front row at the Clements Ribeiro show at a ballroom on Bloomsbury Square, London, 16 February 2013. You don't need a map or an app when finding these shows, just follow girls with the legs of flamingos wearing difficult shoes. There is a man in a fur biker helmet carrying a man bag. At Topshop tomorrow, I will be herded into a dank corner of Tate Modern behind a barrier to wait among young women who could be my daughters, but of course they are not, because I have always been working and starving. Starving and working. At Donna Karan in New York the week before, I was told by the PRs I did not have a seat for the show, and I was to go and stand by a wall in a corner. I cried. It is always thus, these days, now I no longer edit a glossy, and now I am always so critical of fashion, so disappointed. Here is my review of the Victoria Beckham show on 11 September 2012:

You would think, given it was the eleventh of September and I was in Manhattan, that I was a man sporting a beard with something suspicious taped to my waist given my reception at the top of the stairs to the New York Public Library. At 10am, on a hot and sunny Sunday, which made everyone a bit fractious as we were all already in Winter

2012, I was faced with a barrage of blonde harridans wielding clipboards and walkie talkies. These were Victoria Beckham's henchwomen, and they obviously had been shown my photo as the Least Wanted person on their long list. They made me wait to one side. They told me I was blocking the entrance, which is odd as I'm a size 8. The great and good of fashion – except *Vogue* editors Anna Wintour and Alex Shulman, who surprisingly hadn't bothered to show; Beckham is not this week's hottest ticket, btw. Like the disc in her back, her status has slipped to below that of Tom Ford – stomped past me in their giant shoes. I was pushed to one side by super stylist Rachel Zoe's 'people', which meant I was officially fashion roadkill.

Why was I barred from Victoria's show? Well, I have been critical about the fact she uses so much snake skin and crocodile skin in her accessories. As a Spice Girl, she famously refused to wear fur. Now, she makes £14,000 handbags out of a creature who, if it's a snake, is pumped with water while it's still alive to loosen the skin, or if it's a crocodile is pole-axed repeatedly. I accused her of only being interested in money, not ethics: as a pop star she eschewed fur not through morality, but so as not to put off the young girls who bought her records. Now, she wants the super-rich idiots who buy her wares to feel this label is somehow exclusive and out of the reach of mere mortals.

But, no matter how many shows I've been barred from

over the years (I get the same treatment from Burberry, Marc Jacobs, Ralph Lauren, Louis Vuitton, Jonathan Saunders, Christopher Kane, Erdem, Mary Katrantzou, even Paul Smith), it still smarts. I was near tears. I almost emailed Victoria's right-hand woman and promised that, this time, I would give her boss a good review. But I managed to stop myself. To do so would make me as corruptible as all the other members of the fashion press. I tried to get critiques of the show as the crowd left, but everyone was scared to talk to me in case they 'fell out of favour' when it came to getting their discount. 'It was beee-yoooo-ti-fulll!' was about the sum of my *vox pop.* 'Victoria didn't talk us through the collection, she barely took a bow at the end, but she's probably ex*haus*ted!' was another useful insight from a woman on $1m a year with a town car and chauffeur thrown in.

Ah well. I have looked at the clothes backstage and online, and here is what VB thinks you should be wearing next spring. Long, black leather leggings that will inevitably sag at the knees after just one wear, but who cares as this crowd only wears things once. Flat sandals, which one editor told me was, 'So brave! Victoria can't wear heels because of her back!' Oh, the courage! The people mourning at Ground Zero have nothing on this lot. Shoulders are the new erogenous zone because, honestly, what is the point of Pilates if no one sees them, skirts finish mid-thigh, and the colour of choice has moved from nude to off-white or, as my American fashion blogger acquaintance told me, 'putty'. There were lots of blousons and VB's signature, the Exposed

Zip. There were a couple of beautiful (sorry, beee-yoooo-ti-fulll!) dresses: a coral halter neck with grey military detailing, a pale, chiffon, drop-waist shift with embroidery, and two hour-glass columns that will surely be snapped up for the red carpet (there were no stars present on Sunday morning, bar Anna Dello Russo, a woman with skin the colour of cake parchment, and who was wearing a lampshade). But of course it was all about the bags: giant beasts that the current model of the moment, Arizona Muse, struggled to lift, given her arms are mere saplings, honed only by lifting a Champagne flute to those perfect lips. The oddest item was a Beatles cap, with patent leather trimming, worn with almost every outfit. And, of course, there were no trousers, or real tailoring of any kind, probably because VB hasn't yet completed that part of her design degree. No, she is still at the 'wrapping fabric around me' stage. She has not one original idea of her own.

As I descended the New York library steps, the fount of so much knowledge, one of those edgy idiots from the style press, dressed in head to toe paisley pyjamas, said to her companion, 'That was so moving. The two minutes silence at the beginning to honour the dead. The whole new sporty direction. The butteryness of the palette.' The funniest moment was when *Harper's Bazaar* editor Glenda Bailey said she was so happy Victoria had named her new daughter after her magazine. But maybe she wasn't joking. Honestly, I don't think I can do this anymore.

EPILOGUE

It would be easy to type that I haven't changed fashion since I first dipped my toe in its murky pond all those years ago when I gazed at Janice Dickinson's perfect face on the cover of *Vogue*. But, in fact, not only have I not changed it, it has got worse. The smallest, therefore biggest, model right now is Karlie Kloss, who has a 22-inch waist and was once rumoured to have been admitted to a clinic to combat an eating disorder. We have that last thing in common, I suppose. There is still the same level of obfuscation, of denial, that there ever was. I am as outside fashion now as I was outside Olympic gymnastics when I stood in the sports hall of Brentwood High in my navy blue shorts, baulking at the vaulting horse, unable to get off the ground when climbing the rope.

And what of me? Am I happier, saner, fatter, fitter? I took part in a self-help session with a group of eight other women not long ago. The type of therapy, and I have tried many, was called 'wantology': it was all about getting what you want. But after ages of talking and drawing my fantasy coat of arms and answering quizzes, I became angry. 'I am still no closer to getting what I want!' I shouted, to everyone's amazement. 'And you!' I said, pointing to a 30-year-old blonde with big tits and huge ambition – you know, your basic nightmare – 'You should not draw a diamond engagement ring in your personal coat of arms because, if you get married, your husband will betray you, then want half your money and half your house!' Has she not heard of the no-fault divorce? I am always wishing, with every fibre of my being, that I could travel back in time to a point, ooh, I don't know, when I was five maybe, and change everything. But I can't do that. 'But you can time travel forward,' said your basic nightmare. 'You can look forward and imagine how you want your life to be.' Even if I imagine, now, what I want – to be at peace on my horse, a collie at my side, an image I have drawn many times in psychotherapy sessions – it's an image that is always tinged at the edges with worry, like a stain: will the collie run off and be shot by an angry farmer; will the horse shy at a car or a leaf, take off and die; will I die? It's a difficult pattern to break. My husband once said that I'm incapable of being happy, and I think he was right: it's an illness, like herpes.

So. What have I learned that I wish I had known at the

start of this book? That if you drive your car through water you will bugger the engine. That you should moisturise your T-zone, even if you have acne, otherwise you will have a chin that is wrinkly, like sand when the tide is out. Diptyque candles should be placed in the freezer overnight before lighting. That credit cards are poison, as are some people. That you should never shave your legs or pluck your eyebrows or veneer your teeth. And while your eyebrows will never recover from having been a Sara Moon arc, perversely, if you pluck a hair from your chin, seven will come to its funeral. That there are no happy endings. That you should open all envelopes that arrive at your house, particularly brown ones with the words 'Please open immediately' on the front, not stuff them in a drawer. That you can have cellulite, even if you have a BMI of 8. That no dress is worth £2,000 (the most expensive item I have ever bought is a black cashmere Jil Sander duster coat, bought in a rush at Barneys in LA for £3,600 so that I could cover my arms while covering the Oscars). That I should have saved and taken out a pension. That interest-only mortgages are not a good idea, nor is employing builders without a written quotation.

That I should never have got married to a man a friend once described as polyamorous, but actually I think was just borderline autistic or, as his best man later told me, '70 per cent gay'. Not just because of the expense and the heartbreak, but because I am not cut out to live so closely to another human being: it's just too exhausting and disillusioning. Looking at my wedding photos, I realise that of all the guests there that day, I am only in touch with one friend: Sue Needleman, of Montgenèvre-hell-hole fame. That is pretty damning, isn't it? Not my husband, not his best man, not my best man, not even Kerry, who damn nearly came on the honeymoon: she has disappeared, busy with her family. (I phoned Kerry's office once, secretly, furtively, not saying who I was, to ask her deputy editor on the magazine where she now works whether Kerry was okay. I'd sent so many texts with no response, I was worried. 'Oh, yes,' she said perkily, 'she's absolutely fine.') Not Michelle, my Ferretti-clad deputy. Not Robi, my diminutive friend from *The Sunday Times*. Not Beverley. Not Allegra, who I later found out dumped me as a friend because I had written in a column that I had vomited on my plate at her dinner party due to the fact she had put bacon in the supposedly vegetarian lentils, then swished my mouth with water, and emptied the mouthful back into my glass, much to the amazement of the assembled Euro Trash. How unlike *Sex and the City* real life is, I think, as I watch endless re-runs late at night, unable to sleep. Carrie never got into trouble over what she wrote in her weekly column in the *New York Star*. When Big demurred once when she wanted him to have sex, she merely said, 'It's fiction. Fiction! I embellished.' That excuse never washed with me.

I have learned that you have to have a life: it cannot be all about work. If it is all about work and you achieve success, those close to you will hate you for it, unless your success is showered upon their heads in the form of gifts. Actually, even if you do shower people with gifts, they simply want more.

I have learned that no one cares if you work hard. So many times I have sent in copy, searing copy, where my heart is on my sleeve because disaster has struck, a pet has died, or I know that by writing what I have just written there will be a tremendous fallout of almost nuclear proportions, and all I get in reply is an emailed, 'Thanks Liz!'

I thought diffusing my life through a typewriter or laptop somehow made it okay. That if I suffered, if I slept on the streets, or was made homeless (I'm about to be – Amit my accountant has just emailed to tell me that HMRC are moving to make me bankrupt), or was cheated on, or had my credit card snipped in two in front of me, that at least it made good copy, that I would meet my deadline and fill up those column inches. But now? I'm not so sure. I wouldn't do it all again. I wouldn't roll over when I was sacked as editor, or send my husband on yoga retreat holidays in Ibiza. I would have demanded so much more.

The face lift and blepharoplasty and the assignments to have my legs wrapped in bandages and sea mud, to walk in a murky pool atop Capri, to have the fat from my thighs injected into the backs of my hands, and on and on and on, have made me, if not hated, taken less seriously as a writer. When I was assigned to cover the famine in Somalia in 2012, a rather genius piece of commissioning, if you ask me – a bit like when *The Sunday Times Magazine* sent AA Gill, a restaurant critic, to cover the starvation in Sudan – the *Guardian* ran a piece attacking me for going. But who would they have sent? I wondered, smarting. Should we measure the BMI of a reporter at the same time as we x-ray her shoes at the airport? Should we ask, first, how much she gives to charity? But when from the age of five you have no self-worth, and you then spend your life gazing at the glossy pages of *Vogue*, it's no wonder you think it's okay for people to take things from you, criticise you, ridicule you. I got to the point, not long after I lost out on that lifesaving £300,000 TV deal, when I was driving 220 miles back to Somerset late at night and saw a tree hurtling towards me in the darkness, because I had momentarily fallen asleep at the wheel, that I almost didn't bother to save myself. I thought, in that flash, 'Ah, well. Who cares?'

I no longer diet, not really. Although I would never eat a Mars bar, or a whole banana. I no longer jog and ex, although I still pluck and tan: I suppose that is a 50 per cent improvement. But I know what I ate yesterday, what I will eat today, and what I will eat tomorrow. Abstinence has become a way of life, a way of being. I don't know how to overindulge. I live on adrenaline. I tried to take up drinking on Millennium Eve, the most important night of the century, dating wise, when I had been stood up by the man I was then chasing after. Instead of coming to have dinner with me, and even though I made him the music critic of *Marie Claire*, he wanted to 'see the fireworks on the Embankment with a friend'. You see, even when I pay men, they don't have sex with me. I must operate the worst casting couch in the world. Think of Useless Boyfriend Number Two, he of the high-waisted trousers and TCP for aftershave. Think of my husband, who would rather have sex with women who never give him a single thing. (I even bought a BMW convertible to encourage my husband to go to Sainsbury's and he used it to cruise for women with one of his friends. He spoiled the effect, rather, by ringing me late one night and asking, 'Hey, Lizzie. How do you switch on the headlights?')

Men eschew me for vague, crowded, cold, uncomfortable outings with a mate, or sex with a woman who wears a broderie anglaise maxi skirt and has bad grammar. (My ex-husband's mistress, of course I mean her. She also possessed little self-awareness. Take this email to him: 'I'm thinking of working for an NGO. I'm finding it hard to work out at the gym every day with my current job.') But, unlike my sisters Clare and Lyn, and Sue, to some extent, who at least got a baby out of her transaction with a man, I'm not very good at flirting or at drinking. I always think of the calories. I can drink half a bottle, at a push, never a whole one. I worry about what the alcohol might do to my skin, given the face lift and the Botox and the filler and the IPL and the microdermabrasion and the unguents at £300 a pop. I still use a Sisley serum every day, a product you are only supposed to use after trauma, such as childbirth or a house fire. I wonder if I have gone through the menopause, as there were no female hormones to dry up in the first place; another female rite of passage I have somehow missed out on, like the School Run and owning self-raising flour and lining a baking tray with greaseproof paper. I sometimes wonder whether I will still be having Brazilian waxes when I'm 60: will I even be able to hoist my legs, pretzel fashion, over my still-over-dyed head? I can type that I hope 60 is the new 50, because I invented that analogy. But, seriously, as I tell the young women in Space.NK who are desperately trying to sell me face cream and ask politely what skin type I have: 'Frankly, my dear, I'm a husk.' All those years of trying to make it, to be better than I am; years I have always and only ever counted in column inches.

ACKNOWLEDGEMENTS

Thank you to Maggie Goodman, for giving me my first job on a glossy magazine. I'm sorry I was so useless, and Adam Ant never came through. Thanks also to David Robson, who didn't sack me despite my run-in with a soon-to-be-murdered fashion designer. To Kerry Smith, who translated for me at endless meetings, and kept me sane at both *Marie Claire* and the *Evening Standard.* To my agent, Robert Caskie, and Isabel Evans at PFD. To Nicola Bebb for her fact checking and support. To Sue Peart for continuing to employ me as the Back Passage, Sue Needleman for being a great best friend and never grilling me about what exactly happened in the hell hole with Albert, Dawn Bartlett for reading the first draft and giving it to me straight, and to Rita Lewis, for giving me the job at *Marie Claire* and proving to me there is a big world out there, and that I could not hide forever behind my desk. And, of course, to Carly Cook and Jo Whitford at Simon & Schuster, and Jo Roberts-Miller for enduring the endless rewrites, the cries of 'I just don't know whether anyone will be interested.' I'm sorry if you weren't, but thank you if you were.